Black Belt of the Mind

A Conscious Approach to a Magnificent Life

Dr. Fred Grosse

Published by

Conscious Wealth Press

ISBN 0-977-4454-0-2
Published by: Conscious Wealth Press
               P.O. Box 80010
               Phoenix, AZ 85060

Printed in the United States of America

First Edition Second Printing

Dedication

For Victoria

Acknowledgements

This book is really the distillation of lessons and wisdom I have gathered from so many mentors, teachers and other incarnate angels whose lives have crossed my path. It is not possible to list every name and, if you're reading this, you're probably one of them. For the privilege of sharing life's joys and challenges with you, I am truly grateful.

My love and thanks to my parents, Ruth and Pat Grosse, who at 95 years continue to amaze me with their clarity and generous ability to share, by example, their understanding of what makes a Magnificent Life. To my teachers at Hebrew Union College who provided me with a Renaissance education. Miriam and Irv Polster, masters in the art of Gestalt Therapy, that provided the foundation for much of my life's work. Brugh Joy, you continue to inspire me with your radiance of wisdom and appreciation for the mystery of life. To my son David Aaron, for being there and for sharing your own wisdom with me.

So many of my clients, fellow travelers on this road of self discovery, had the courage to look within and share from the depths of their beings and in doing so taught me much from their leaps in understanding. My thanks to all of you who have urged me over the years to get to work and write it down and then indeed held me accountable to my own commitments.

To Patrick Lilly, my special appreciation, for holding my feet to the fire and offering your insights on my manuscript. Siimon Reynolds, my thanks for your generous support. Cathrin Stewart and Magnolia Ben, thank you for your love and understanding and for sharing your insights with me on my first drafts. Ralph Kamon, my lifelong friend and amazing "older brother" that I always wanted to have—my special appreciation for your encouragement and counsel over the years. Harry Obedin, your staunch support and "how's the book coming along?" over the years have been an ongoing source of encouragement to me. Thank you.

I have immense appreciation for my support team of angels—Suzy de Lautour, Jane Bussey, Mia McMeeken and Samantha Karaitiana—thank you for being the wind under my wings all these years.

My friends call me a verbal fellow (sometimes even, verbose). I'm most comfortable speaking and allowing what wants to come through me to flow through as the spoken word. So, when the question of a book kept coming up, the discipline required to sit down at a computer felt like more than I could handle alone. This book would not have happened without the tireless help, patience and abilities of Joy Atkin. Thank you, Joy.

To Sherry Folb my heartfelt appreciation for the amazing way in which you pulled everything together through your masterful editing and managing of this project. You really did bring it all together for me.

And to Victoria, my beloved, it's a privilege, honor and delight to be married to you. You continue to amaze me with your wisdom, insight, perception and beauty.

Thank you.

Table of Contents

Introduction 9

Chapter One—Life by Accident or Life on Purpose?........................... 11

Chapter Two—Meet Your Soul Mate 29

Chapter Three—The Magnificent Life...45

Chapter Four—Making Dreams Come True 63

Chapter Five—Channels of Consciousness...77

Chapter Six—Mastering the Channels 97

Chapter Seven—Beliefs about Wealth... 113

Chapter Eight—Wealth Consciousness 125

Chapter Nine—Sacred Living.. 143

Chapter Ten—Get a Life—A Magnificent One 155

Appendices

    1: Accountability Checklist.. 166

    2: Dollar-Productive Behavior I 167

    3: Dollar-Productive Behavior II 168

    4: Sample Day Sheet... 169

    5: Ideal Day Sheet 170

    6: Personal Goal Sheet 171

    7: Business Goal Sheet.. 172

    8: Commitment Sheet 173

    9: Time Log 174

Introduction

I want to share something with you right now before we go any further—the most important aspect of this book has very little to do with what you're about to read—it has everything to do with what you write about yourself, what you think, and what you feel as you read. This is especially important when you work with the exercises at the end of each chapter. As you stretch yourself internally and test your capacity to discern what's right and discard what's not appropriate for you, you will find yourself assuming a new level of responsibility for the shape of your life. This is what I call mastery—or **Black Belt of the Mind**—when you are able to call upon your inner resources to create the life for which you yearn.

You see, my purpose in writing a book is not so much to expound my philosophy or to try to convince you of anything, as to move you to look inside yourself and explore—what you think and where you stand on the ideas that I'll be sharing with you.

It is my belief that we are immortals posted to this planet for an experience called life. A Magnificent Life and its recipe are unique to each of us. For the short period of time we have on earth, we have a specific path to follow, weaving our passions, talents and purpose for being here into a tapestry that is an expression of who we are. My hope is that you will enter totally into the game and set aside time to work with your Soul—which is that part of you that leaves when you die—and design and live a life of magnificence that most nurtures and unfolds who you fully are.

I'm going to ask you to read these pages through the eyes of your heart—your transducer of wisdom—and to pay attention when you feel a spark within. This spark may be an indication that you've just come across a phrase that resonates for you, or to which you find yourself reacting, because you know that something is not your point of view.

Read on and keep your internal antennae focused. This is about discovering where a Magnificent Life might take you and what new habits you might need to put in place to achieve this—then to release that which has been keeping you from your destiny. I want you to hang out with the Universe in such a way that you feel fulfilled on a daily basis, knowing that you're living your life.

Over the years I have met many people who, on the material level, had almost everything a human being could desire—a great job, retirement income, and all the toys that western civilization has to offer. And yet they felt a sense of hollowness, that there had to be something more to life. What was missing for them? In my explorations through the years, I found that this gaping hole they so often described had to do with a yearning for a sense of purpose and direction. Often it was a deep fear of getting to the end of their days and experiencing a feeling of having wasted the gift of life.

My deepest hope is that as you read the following pages you will start to feel the inklings of the elements that give your life its richest meaning. It's time for you to meet the authentic you and start creating your own Magnificent Life out of the clues, the inklings and the messages from the insights that come to you.

How will you get the most out of this book? I encourage you to purchase a journal and to commit to recording your responses and reactions to what you're about to read. Do the exercises at the end of each chapter and perhaps encourage your life partner or good friends to have a go as well. This gives you the opportunity to talk about what comes up for you.

As you go about your daily life and thoughts come up, write them down. Become a Black Belt of your own Mind as you go within and look for the teachings and meanings in the events of your life. When we are truly ready, transformation can take only seconds. The key is to be awake to the clues when they present themselves. So often these come in the most simple, commonplace events, such as a pause in conversation over coffee with a friend or suddenly witnessing the red of the daybreak sky. I wish you well on your journey of exploration of what a Magnificent Life is for you—and honing the tools you have to create it.

Dr. Fred

1

Life by Accident or Life on Purpose?

"As far as we can discern, the sole purpose of human existence is to kindle a light of meaning in the darkness of mere being." Carl Jung

Life by Accident

Here you are. You are a human being living on planet earth. You have been living this thing called human life for some time now, maybe 30, 40, 50 or more years. Do you feel like you have it right yet? Or does it somehow feel like no matter what you try, it is more like your life is a series of random occurrences or accidents?

Chances are that if you have picked up this book it feels like some aspects of your life aren't working. Maybe you have made a lot of money and along the way you have lost the love and respect of the person or people you care most about in the world. Or maybe success in your chosen field has always eluded you. Perhaps you have battled with excess weight all your life and no matter what you try, you simply can't lose it and keep it off. Or perhaps you have just retired from full-time work and suddenly you have a lot of leisure and life has lost its lustre.

So where are you going wrong? How come your life feels like just "doing life," a jail sentence that you are trudging through day after day? You ask yourself, "When do I get to be happy?" And, you wonder how come other people seem to be having a lot more fun than you.

It feels like you are on a treadmill, an endlessly boring struggle that, despite your efforts, seems to get harder rather than better. Every week seems a repetition of the one before. You wake up, go to work, come home, take the kids to sports practice, make dinner, clean up, fall into bed, sleep, and start all over again. It often appears that other people—your boss, your clients, and even your loved ones—have more say over how you spend your time and energy than you do.

If you recently retired you may find yourself waking up each morning and wondering how you can possibly fill the day—a day that stretches out in front of you like an eternity. Even if you manage to keep busy that day what about all the days that follow? Perhaps you think back to those productive years and wonder if your brain will turn to mush now that you no longer have the stimulation and challenge of a career. You may feel a sense of wistfulness. It may even feel that you are losing control of your life and that you are walking around in a semi-comatose state—just going through the motions. My sense is that the loss that you feel is the loss of purpose, direction and forward momentum. It can feel like you are almost invisible and nothing you do is of value to anyone. You know you need to find a new purpose for your life, so how do you go about it?

It is my hope that **Black Belt of the Mind** will offer some clues and guidance as to how you might create new passions in your life by choosing each day to live a Magnificent Life—designed just for you, by you. Wouldn't it feel wonderful to get to the end of your life and feel like you had **done it all**—everything you had hoped for, with no regrets?

If Only

If only life came with an instruction manual. Wouldn't that be great? After all, when you buy a new washing machine or computer you get instructions on how to use it. They might not be clearly expressed or well written; however, at least they offer some clues about where to get started. Life, on the other hand, doesn't come with a personalized manual. You came naked and defenseless into the world and it may feel like you have struggled ever since.

You do have a guidance system consisting of the DNA genetic coding with which you were born, the guidance and opinions offered by your parents that reflected their life experience, and the enculturation process of education and socialization. This generic framework has probably enabled you to operate within the mentality of your particular society. My question to you is, "When does the individual that you are, with all your hopes, desires, dreams, talents and skills, get the opportunity to express him- or herself authentically?"

Black Belt of the Mind

If nature gives every acorn a blueprint telling it how to grow into an oak tree and every snowflake its own unique design, how come human beings don't have instructions on how to be the individuals that they are? How come Joe doesn't get a blueprint on the day he is born telling him how to be Joe? It just doesn't make sense, does it?

You're right. It doesn't. There is *no way* nature would have made such a blunder. I'm here to tell you that life *does* come with a built-in partner, a map, and a compass.

Think of this book as your personalized guidebook. It can help you identify those aspects of yourself that, up until now, may have been redundant, like the spare parts that come with a computer.

Consider this: When you started up your computer it seemed to work just fine. Since you didn't really know what those spare parts did, you probably left them in the box and put the box in a closet. You also put the manuals in the same box just in case something went wrong. You promptly forgot about them and went about your business. After some time you realize your computer is getting slower and slower. You suddenly remember that box of spare parts and it occurs to you that perhaps you should find the box—dust off the parts and read the manual.

Well, in terms of your life, you have been like that computer. Sure, you have been functioning to some degree up until now, but what if I were to tell you that all this time you have been running at a fraction of your real potential?

What if I could show you that your own built-in spare parts have tremendous power to transform you and every aspect of your existence—as long as you take them out of the closet and start using them? Why continue to be less than you are? Today is the day that you need to find those spare parts, dust them off, and read the manual to see how they might improve your internal computer and your own Inner Wisdom. This can move you into Black Belt mastery of your own life.

You, Plus Three Helpers

I believe that you are never alone. You actually have three built-in helpers—your Soul, your Unique Psychological Fingerprint (UPF) and your heart. With decision, commitment, practice and accountability, you can work in beautiful harmony with your partners, empowering you to live life to the **Power of Three**.

Soul Partner

Everyone has a potential partner dwelling within. This partner is called your **Soul**. Your Soul longs to be your life partner and until you decide to give it the job, it is a bit like the employee who has no work to do, who is sitting around getting bored and, sooner or later, becomes disenchanted.

You see, human beings have been given free will. Your Soul needs direction and until you give it—it is nothing more than a passenger sitting in the back seat of the vehicle that is travelling through the journey of your life. My purpose is to reintroduce you to your Soul and help you become partners in this business of living life on purpose. If you make a commitment to marry your Soul Partner in this lifetime and adopt these techniques, you may find your mission and then be able to create it. Every day you will be focused on your destiny and purpose, and your life will have a sense of yes-ness about it.

Unique Psychological Fingerprint

So now you know you don't have to travel this journey alone. It gets better! Not only do you have a Soul Partner, you also have a blueprint, just like the snowflake and acorn. Have you ever broken open an acorn to see what gives it its acorn-ness? The brown dust inside the shell is its genetic coding, the DNA blueprint that tells it how to grow into an oak tree.

You, too, have your own blueprint for life. I call this blueprint or inner map your **Unique Psychological Fingerprint (UPF)**. Your UPF is the combination of things that make up your natural inclinations; the things that you love so much that they come easy. It is actually the area or areas of your life where you are a genius. In all my years of working with people I have never met anyone who didn't have an area of genius.

We have been conditioned to believe that geniuses are the top five percent who rank highest on IQ tests—actually you can be a genius in many ways. Some people can make an apple pie that is so delicious that those who eat it swoon with delight. Other people are gifted at organizing, others at public speaking, still others are geniuses at making the engine of a car sing. Some people are geniuses at smiling in such a way that the person receiving the smile feels blessed. Genius, by my definition, is about people being in harmony with their UPF and expressing it in the fullest way.

Because no one else is the same as you, your UPF is different from that of your sister, your neighbor, me, even your child (which is something I often have to remind parents). You may not, at this point, know what your UPF is. That's OK. As you read on and work through the exercises, my hope is that you will discover the unique genius that is you, which the world is waiting to receive. Ask yourself each morning and evening, "What is my unique gift?" Or, "What is the treasure that has been put in my cradle as my birthright?" Move yourself into a place of openness and nonjudgement and perhaps let that still, small voice inside whisper some suggestions to you.

Read With Your Heart

Last but not least, you have a compass that, if consulted, will always steer you in the right direction. That compass is your **heart**. I want to encourage you to use your heart when reading this book rather than your intellect. Your intellect is a wonderful thing; however, when addressing matters of spirit, your mind can get in the way because it is only used to working with logic. If you want to get the most out this experience, I suggest you read with your heart. It will tell you whether or not this information is true for you.

How will you know if you are engaging your heart or your intellect? Quite simply, you will feel a heart agreement with the things that resonate for you. For me, when I hear or read something that feels true and important, it often takes the form of a physical sense of warmth in my heart area or more specifically in the heart energy center of my body—which is in the middle of the chest just above the sternum.

On the other hand, if you are still filtering things through your intellect, you may hear that negative voice that tells you this is all too hard and it won't work. For the moment, I suggest that you suspend the inner critic and allow the possibilities of what I'm suggesting to be felt at the deeper heart level.

Who Am I Really?

Have you ever stood in front of a mirror and wondered who you really are? There are many words to choose from that may describe you, for instance, *teenager, middle-aged man, menopausal woman, lover, husband, wife, father, mother, son, daughter, grandmother, salesperson, company director, millionaire, retiree, senior citizen, tennis player, churchgoer, piano player, skier* and so on—these are really just labels. They are names for different aspects of you—roles you perform in society such as being a caring son or daughter to your aging parents, or terms used to describe different interests that you have, such as playing tennis or the piano.

Our society likes to classify and label people—just be aware that you have a choice whether or not to accept these descriptions. In the exercise that follows, you are going to experience—albeit briefly—how it might feel to let go of the limitations, restrictions and expectations inherent in these definitions of who you are.

Imagine that you are standing in front of that mirror and like a snake shedding its skin—all those labels are falling onto the floor. They are just skins that, for now, you have discarded. Imagine they are in a big pile beside you, waiting for when you decide to put them back on.

Personality Plus—Which One Is Me?

Have another look in the mirror. How does it feel to be free of all those labels? Some of them carry a lot of expectation and responsibility. How does it feel to be temporarily free? Perhaps you feel lighter. Perhaps you feel frightened. Whatever it is you feel at this point, just notice what you are feeling.

When you are ready, let's go back to our question, "Who am I?" We have established that you are not the roles you play, so what does that leave? What about the multifaceted aspects of your personality?

Swiss psychologist Carl Jung (1875-1962) coined the term sub-personality. According to Jung, every one of us has at least 70 different personalities or selves residing within us. You will have your own list of sub-personalities but they may include the Procrastinator, Perfectionist, Worrier, Judge, Comedian, Pusher, Cynic, Guilty Person, Catastrophizer, Blamer and Skeptic.

So which sub-personality is the real **you**? Perhaps you are a self-assured businessman who runs his company very successfully and a fun-loving dad who plays ball with his kids. At the same time you might occasionally turn into an aggressive driver who won't let anyone pass you on the freeway.

Or maybe you are a successful career woman who is also an enthusiastic and playful lover. You might also be a mom who loves to read stories to her kids at bedtime, an angry wife who insults her husband when she's feeling neglected, or a passive daughter who lets her mother tell her she is sacrificing her family for her career.

Every one of us has a multitude of sub-personalities to call on in any given situation. Some make us feel happy and others don't. So which one describes who you really are? The word personality really defines a set of behaviors, roles and aspects of you rather than your true essence. Imagine that those sub-personalities, the ones you like and the ones you don't, are also falling onto the floor at your feet. Look again in the mirror. What else do you see?

A Body by Any Other Name

You see a body. It has a particular shape. You are tall or short, fat or thin. Your hair may be brown, blonde, red, or gray. Your eyes are blue, green, or brown. Within these broad classifications there are countless variations. Your eyes may be a combination of green and brown that can be called hazel. Your hair may be called brunette, but if you look closely at the individual hairs they range in color from dark brown to gold.

Our outer bodies or vessels come in many shapes and sizes and this is the awe-inspiring diversity of mankind. If we all looked the same, the world would be a pretty boring place and, what's more, it would be difficult to identify our loved ones from everyone else.

Your looks are unique—does this mean that your body is who you really are? Aren't "short," "brunette" or "blue-eyed" simply more labels? Don't they describe how you look, rather than being roles you perform or interests you have?

It is true that many of us link our happiness to our looks and this is reinforced if others find us attractive. Society and the media encourage this. In fact, there is an obsession with youth and looks that is really a conspiracy to sell more products and services. Advertisements would have you believe that if you could just lose those wrinkles, extra pounds or gray hair, everything would be wonderful. Would it really? It is certainly true that by improving how you appear to the world you will probably feel better about yourself and, with activation of your sub-personalities of self-confidence and self-esteem, your inner world might also improve.

If this is all it takes to find meaning in life and be truly happy, why do most people who lose weight with an intensive diet or exercise program simply put it all back on again after a few months?

Often, it is because they have done nothing to change their belief structure about who they are. When their body changes shape, it may be threatening for them to be seen in a new way or challenging for their family because it shows that change is possible. When people come under this sort of unconscious internal or external pressure, they often decide unconsciously that things felt more comfortable before, so they allow the old habits to resurface and take over again like an untended lawn where the weeds soon grow back.

Are You Your Age, Weight or Shoe Size?

Young or old, fat or thin, aren't you much more than a sum of your age and body parts?

The undeniable truth of this is vividly illustrated by the condition known as Alzheimer's disease. The tragedy of Alzheimer's is really the torment suffered by the patient's partner, family, and friends. They have to come to terms with the fact that the body of the person they love is still present, with the same way of moving, speaking, smiling, and gesturing. Yet within that familiar shell, no one is home. The Alzheimer's victim can look at their spouse of 40 years or a cherished child and have no idea who they are. It is as if the Soul has gone into suspended animation.

When you go to a funeral, you witness a body from which the Soul has passed on. The body still looks the same as it did just before death—in fact, if we were to weigh it a minute before death and a minute afterwards, we would discover it still weighed exactly the same—yet the essence of the person is gone. It is the weightless, invisible, immortal Soul presence that has departed and is mourned by family and friends.

So, you are not your body and you are not your labels or personality. I ask again, *"Who are you?"* Continue looking in the mirror in your imagination. Now pretend you are unzipping your body and stepping out of it. There it is—your head, torso, arms and legs all falling away. It is just a suit you wear each day and now it is at your feet beside the labels and personalities you discarded previously.

I'd Like You to Meet—Your Soul Partner

What is left? Who is this being who lives inside your body?

You are a Soul, an incarnate angel, here on earth having an experience of life as a human being. I often use a German word, *geist*, to describe the Soul because it has no religious overtones. Geist is the unique combination of your hopes, beliefs, attitudes, dreams, feelings, and life experience; everything that expresses your spirit. It is your evolved software package that develops with you over time.

Look again in the mirror. Can you see this geist or human spirit? No, because the real you is actually invisible to most of us. In our society we might think that if something is invisible it must not exist, yet every day we experience thoughts, ideas, and feelings. Are they visible? No. I'm sure you will agree they do exist. In fact, even medical science acknowledges our thoughts can be so powerful they can make us sick or heal us.

Let's compare the Soul to the element wind. Wind is also invisible, yet it has force, direction, and humidity as any sailor can tell you after a day sailing on the harbor. It can also be felt, measured, and harnessed. The human spirit is composed of hopes, dreams, attitudes, beliefs, and life experience. Like wind—geist has texture. It can be shaped and influenced. The particular combination of those qualities that are within you is what makes you, **you**—instead of your next-door neighbor or the guy who owns the deli down the road, or even your father, mother or brother.

Another word for this is essence. Essence means the intrinsic nature of something or its flavor. Imagine drinking coffee that didn't have a unique bitter flavor and distinctive aroma, or eating chocolate that had had the entire chocolate flavor removed. Neither one would taste very good. They wouldn't have the effect on your sensory system—activating your taste-buds and salivary glands—that the mere smell of coffee and chocolate usually evokes. The essence of you comprises the things that give you your own individual flavor.

The Meaning of Life–Using Our Heart as a Compass

When I was at Seminary studying to be a Rabbi, I studied Greek mythology. One of my favorite stories is the legend of Prometheus and how he gave human beings the secret of fire.

Until that time, fire had been regarded as proprietary information and only the Gods and Goddesses had known about its importance and uses. Man had been kept in his place, condemned to live like the beasts, eating raw meat and sheltering in caves.

Prometheus, a Titan, had deep sympathy for the plight of humankind. He decided to defy Zeus and give humans the gift of fire, knowing full well that he would suffer for his actions.

When Zeus heard what the compassionate Prometheus had done, he was livid. Not only had Prometheus disobeyed him—and for that he would be punished—but Zeus knew that now that humans had fire, it was possible that they might discover other knowledge only known by the deities.

In particular, there was one piece of information to which humans must never be privy. Zeus immediately convened a meeting on Mount Olympus of all the Gods and Goddesses. At this meeting the deities had to decide where this precious information should be hidden.

What was this secret that was so important that it must never be discovered by mere mortals? This secret was far more significant than fire—it was none other than the **Secret to the Meaning of Life**. The deities were united in their belief that human beings simply could not be entrusted with such knowledge. Where could this precious information be concealed? They debated and discussed the possibilities. Should the secret be hidden on a star? What about under the ocean where Neptune could keep an eye on it? Every possible hiding place was suggested and eventually discarded as not being appropriate for such a secret. Was there any place where man would not think to look?

Finally, after much deliberation, someone thought of the perfect place—an absolutely brilliant, foolproof hiding place. The deities decreed that the secret would be hidden in the human heart—because people look outward rather than inward for solutions and direction and no one would think to look there.

What Does Your Heart Tell You?

From my own observations I believe the deities were right. Most people go blindly through life, seldom listening to the deepest longings of their heart from their Soul. Instead they do what they think is expected of them by others—their families, friends, work colleagues, and neighbors—and fill their lives with distractions or addictions.

People often fill their homes with the latest toys that advertisements tell them they should want. To pay for all those designer labels, they have to work harder and longer to make more money. As they work long hours, they tell themselves there is no time to exercise properly or even to take meal breaks. So they grab quick snacks and eat on the run. When they finally get home at night, they are so tired they tell themselves they'll just have one drink to relax. The one drink turns to three and then when they fall into bed exhausted, they can't sleep properly because the alcohol is actually a stimulant and keeps them awake. They toss and turn all night as they worry about the things that happened during the day and all that they have to do tomorrow.

Of course, their beloveds suffer because the workaholic is never really fully present, even when he is at home. He might be physically sitting at the dinner table looking at his wife as she tells him about her day but his mind is elsewhere, wrestling with the difficult decision he has to make about his latest project. Perhaps his wife feels cheated because she knows that her spouse is not honoring her with his full attention and is not available for her attention and affection.

Life on Purpose

On the other hand, living a life of your own design is a completely different ball game. It means defining the things that give you a sense of yes-ness and then putting them firmly in place. This is a way of funding your Magnificent Life—a life that holds true meaning for you.

When I talk about creating a life on purpose, some people say, "Oh, but I like to go with the flow." I agree that going with the flow can be wonderful; however, my question is, "What flow do you mean?"

If you just wake up each morning with no purpose or plan and wait for the day to unfold then you are like a feather blowing in the wind. Like the feather, the prevailing wind currents will determine your direction and you will have no control over where you land. Other people, television, advertising, email, phone calls and a myriad of influences may grab your attention. By the end of the day your time will have been used up. Then the question is, "Will you have achieved anything for you?"

By doing life on purpose, you decide on the dream you want to follow and then create the opportunity for flow. For instance, in my Magnificent Life I plan time to go fishing. I set aside the time in my diary; I arrange transport, hire a guide and make all the necessary preparations. Once I'm on the fishing trip, I am in Universal Time and completely in the flow of the activity of fishing. To me, this is creating life to my own design.

Guided Meditation CD: Birthing the Dream with Victoria Sinclair

You will find this downloadable guided meditation on my website www. drfredgrosse.com—once it's downloaded, you can transfer it to a CD.

Take some quiet time now to listen to the meditation and do the following exercises. You can write in this book or in your journal. These exercises and the meditation CD are designed to reconnect you to the knowledge of who you truly are. They will also stimulate your inner voices, imagination, and dream state.

This meditation will take you on a journey where you may experience your true nature. It is particularly powerful if used first thing in the morning, but feel free to listen to it whenever it suits you best. Please, do not listen to this when driving a car or operating electrical equipment.

Perhaps this is the first time you have done a guided meditation. If so, just find a comfortable place where you will not be disturbed for about 40 minutes. Make sure you are wearing comfortable clothes that do not restrict your movements and that all your physical needs such as hunger, thirst, and so on have been attended to. Either lie down or sit, whatever is more comfortable to you. Close your eyes and simply focus on Victoria's voice.

Know that whatever you experience is perfect for you right now. Relax and enjoy!

Exercise One

After the Meditation

Write down six words or phrases that describe how you are feeling right now.

I feel:

_____

_____

_____

_____

_____

_____

Exercise Two

Towards the end of the guided meditation you remembered that you are a star, a shining light. You recalled that your mission is to go to earth and shine. That simply means that every day your mission is to be who you are, not what anyone else says you should be. You came into this life with unique talents and special gifts. The meditation helped you recall what they are.

Take this quiet moment to remember your mission as it was revealed in the meditation or how you are feeling it right now in your heart. When you are ready you might like to express this in the Sacred Mission Statement that follows.

If the time is not yet right for you to do so, that's fine. You can come back to it when you are ready. Keep working with the meditation and observe what turns up in your life. Know that your Sacred Mission is encoded in your heart. Spending time in quiet contemplation is the only way you will come to know your heart's desire and the unfolding of your Soul Purpose.

My Sacred Mission:

I, _____, am a shining light. My purpose in being on earth is to shine.

My Unique Psychological Fingerprint is

_____

_____

_____

_____

_____

My unique talents and special gifts are

_____

_____

_____

_____

_____

My Soul's calling is

_____

_____

_____

_____

_____

My life path is

_____

_____

_____

_____

_____

Signed _____

Date _____

Exercise Three

Know Thyself

In Chapter One we talked about some of the **Roles** or **Labels** we take on during our lifetime. Until we become conscious and start CHOOSING the roles that suit us, we often find that we have been assigned roles by society and significant others in our lives. Fill in the columns below with all the roles and labels you believe you currently have.

Roles (e.g., wife, lover, grandmother)   **Labels** (e.g., senior citizen)

Exercise Four

Assess the words you have written for Exercise Three. Take a red pen and circle or underline those that no longer suit you. Can you imagine what life might be like without them?

Using a blue pen, circle or underline the roles and labels you enjoy and choose to continue. Are there any more you would like to add to your list—for instance, investor, artist, traveller, or gourmet chef? Can you imagine what life would be like if you became these things? Write four sentences in the space below describing how it would be.

If I was to become

_____

_____

_____

_____

life would be

_____

_____

_____

_____

_____

_____

_____

_____

2

Meet Your Soul Mate

*"Everything that irritates us about others can lead
to an understanding of ourselves." Carl Jung*

Soul Partners

In Chapter One we discovered that we are much more than our physical body and personality. We also discovered that we are not alone. We have a Soul Partner who desires an intimate relationship with us. In this chapter we will explore further the nature of this Soul Partnership and what this might mean for your life. We will also start to put some shape to the Magnificent Life you might want to create.

The Invisible Made Visible

Remember the mirror in the last chapter? Imagine you are back in front of the same mirror and this time you are looking at your Soul. The invisible has become visible. What, if anything, do you see?

Perhaps you see an angel. Perhaps you see light. This light might be white or gold or pink or some other color or combination of colors. Perhaps you don't actually see anything, yet you feel a sense of peace or warmth. Whatever you are experiencing, just let yourself feel it for a few moments. Breathe into this moment.

Does it feel comfortable to be spending time like this in companionship with your Soul? Does it feel easy and effortless? Can you feel how familiar your Soul Partner actually is? Now imagine that the angel or light emerges from the mirror and enfolds you with golden light. You are cocooned in this light as it completely surrounds you. It feels wonderfully loving and protective. Bask in the glow of this feeling for a few seconds.

It is a bit like coming home from work and having your dog rush to the door to greet you. He has missed you while you have been away. He wags his tail and licks your hand. He might bark or even jump up on you. He recognizes you as his loving master or mistress and he wants to tell you how much he loves and appreciates you. The exercises at the end of Chapter One were designed to help you experience the recognition, familiarity, and appreciation that your Soul has for you. Your Soul wants to let you know every day just how loved and appreciated you are.

You can have this feeling each time you check in with your Soul. I want you to get used to checking in every few hours of each day. You might check in at 7am, 10am, 1pm, 3pm, 5pm and so on. It only takes a moment. Simply take a deep breath and ask yourself, "On a scale of 1 to 10, with 10 being optimum, how present am I right now? How aligned am I with my Soul purpose right now?" The more you do this, the stronger your connection with your Soul will be and the more frequently you will notice when you are off track and need to make adjustments to get back on course. I liken this to Air Traffic Control. An aircraft only needs minor adjustments to its flight path to get back on course. These adjustments are frequent and require constant monitoring.

In the Driver's Seat

Are you getting a sense of being in the driver's seat of your life, with your Soul in the passenger seat holding a map, navigating the best route to take? This Soul Partner navigator is so in tune with you and your desires that it can anticipate what you will need next. Like any good navigator, it will suggest, "You might like to move into the far right lane because we need to turn right at the next intersection."

Not only are you in the driver's seat of this vehicle called life with your Soul Partner beside you, the two of you control the shape of your vehicle. In other words, you can decide whether you want to be driving a Ferrari, a BMW, a Honda, or a Pontiac. Do you want a shiny new red one or would you prefer silver? Do you want power under the hood or are you more concerned with the mileage you get from every gallon of gas? Do you want life by design or by accident?

Each day we either consciously decide to achieve certain things or, by default, we abdicate responsibility for the day to outside stimuli. Whether conscious or unconscious, we have significantly more control over our responses to everyday occurrences than most of us use.

Life on purpose means sitting down and designing a Magnificent Life that pleases us. It means planning what we want to do and putting strategies in place to get there. I believe that a Magnificent Life is possible for every single person regardless of caste or intelligence. The attributes required for this include desire, will, commitment, persistence and a willingness to be held accountable. It means putting in place the Eight Point Plan described in detail in Chapter Four.

So we put the plan in place. Does this then mean we have to struggle and toil to make it succeed? Does our Soul then turn into a hard taskmaster, nagging us to constantly do more, more, more, and making us feel guilty when we don't? This is certainly the view of some, but it is not mine. In fact, by harnessing our Soul power I believe we access an awesome force that can be used to manifest our Magnificent Lives. Even the so-called negative energies such as fear can be converted to adrenaline that can then be used as kinetic energy to achieve the goal. For instance, if I am fearful because I know I have to address a conference of a thousand people, I use that nervousness by turning it into adrenaline, which then energizes my speaking performance. It is a matter of realizing that this energy is at our disposal and deciding how best to use it.

Let me tell you more about this amazing power and how you might benefit from having it in your life.

Incarnate Angel

We have been sent here by the Creator to experience what it is to be human, with all the challenges and joys that go along with living on earth. Think about the implications of that for a moment. We are all angelic beings. Our essence is that of the angelic realm. Far from being limited, our birthright is that of the angels. Marianne Williamson expressed it beautifully when she wrote the following words for Nelson Mandela's Inaugural Speech in 1994:

> **You are a child of God**
> **Your playing small does not serve the world.**
> **There's nothing enlightened about shrinking so that other people won't feel insecure around you.**
> **We are born to <u>make manifest the glory of God that is within us.</u>** [Underlining is mine.]

On a practical level what does this mean for your life? Perhaps you are a real estate professional. You can view yourself as a salesperson promoting a deal in order to buy yourself a bigger house, or a newer car, or you can see yourself as an incarnate angel who has been given a divine curriculum in real estate in order to meet and serve unique beings who have been sent to teach you something. If you have this view of your life it can change things mightily, including how you approach others while you are prospecting for listings.

Marianne Williamson says that our birthright is direct access to the glory of God within us to manifest that which we desire in our lives. Far from being the obedient good child of Sunday school days, the Soul actually has a wild, elegant, regal nature that knows no limits.

May the Force Be With You

When that wild nature is harnessed, it can either be for your best interests or it can be a distraction or a way of filling in time before you die. For instance, the Hebrew Bible story of David teaches that David used this power to defeat the mighty Goliath. Using a sling and some stones he defeated an enemy who was far stronger than he. His fearlessness was made possible by harnessing this mighty power. In modern language, the **force** was with him.

Everything in our curriculum is sent to us by the Creator. In mastering his fear of fighting Goliath, David built a skill base to turn himself into a great leader. In developing the hero within, David and many other great heroes throughout history have shown us what is possible. I call this mastery of self, the **Black Belt of the Mind**.

There are many stories of ordinary people who have used this awesome power to perform extraordinary feats—such as the New York City firefighters during the terrorist attacks of 9/11. There are countless other stories of ordinary citizens performing superhuman or selfless acts of bravery during and after 9/11. These people tapped into their inner glory to find extraordinary courage and strength.

In the same way, a mother might find superhuman strength to lift a car crushing her child or jump into rapids to rescue a drowning child. Anything is possible when you learn to tap into that power. It's clear that it does not have to be just a once-in-a-lifetime experience. Although the examples given above are instances of extraordinary feats performed in extraordinary circumstances, this force can be used continually in your life to create that which you desire.

The teenager who gets up at 5am every morning, summer and winter, to train for two hours before school because he has a vision of swimming on the US Olympic Swimming Team has found this power. So has the young girl living in the slums with the crack-addicted mother who gets herself ready for school every day because she dreams of going to a university. She knows that what she does today and tomorrow will create her future and she has found the power within herself to honor her dreams. Both the swimmer and the student are daring to dream the impossible dream. They are so committed to their vision of the future that they are prepared to make all the sacrifices required to get there.

Often we have a Sunday school vision of the Soul as a meek, obedient, goody two shoes. Actually, I believe the reality is quite the opposite. I equate the Soul to the exquisite free-spirited, wild nature of an Arabian horse. If you have ever seen a thoroughbred Arabian steed pawing the ground, bucking its head and flaring its nostrils, you will understand what I mean. Soul power is that untamed exuberance, that barely restrained potency and regal bearing that says, "Don't mess with me; I know where I'm going." Soul power is dynamic and vigorous; a mighty force for change that when harnessed can manifest miracles.

Remember Who You Are

Have you noticed that in all of nature it seems that only human beings need to be reminded of who they are? Look around the next time you are in the garden or out in the countryside. Worms, birds, butterflies, cats, dogs, cows, sheep, goats, horses, plants and flowers all know who and what they are. They simply go about their business of being a worm, cow, plant or flower. There is no struggle involved and I've never seen a cow trying to be a sheep. So why do human beings forget who they are? Why does someone like Joe want to play tennis like Pete Sampras even though he really has a talent for scuba diving? Or, why does Annette wish she could be a great actress like Nicole Kidman when all the children in her preschool class think she is an absolutely wonderful teacher?

As we have already discovered, part of the answer to that question is that the very process of being born a human being involves taking on a denser body that has limitations. In my view, the socialization process and education are designed to confuse us and help us forget our true nature. We are trained to be less than we are, to fit in; to choose certain professions even if they are completely disharmonious with our UPF and our natural talents and skills, simply because others think those professions are our meal ticket to a successful and abundant life, or because it would be a fulfilment of their own dreams.

Transformation in an Instant

It is important to understand that transformation can happen in an instant, even though you may have been preparing for it all your life. In connecting with your heart and Soul as we did in Chapter One, you may have seen the awesome possibilities of what you can create and having experienced that, you have already changed.

On a day-by-day basis it is also possible to transform your mood in an instant. Those who have seen the movie *Sliding Doors* will relate to how one choice can make a difference to an individual's life. Perhaps you have experienced this yourself. You may have met your beloved in a chance meeting because you decided to go to a certain café or restaurant where you happened to run into an old friend having coffee who introduced you to his companions—one of whom you had an instant connection with. Or perhaps you decided to take a certain job, even though it meant relocating to another state and there you met the person who is now the love of your life. Every day we have the potential to change our lives in both big and small ways.

Daily Check-in

Let's explore how to check in with how you are feeling at regular intervals during the day. Using a scale of 1 to 10, with 10 being the optimum, you will rate how you are feeling in any given moment. If the score is very low, for instance, under 5, you can take a moment to breathe deeply and visualize a particularly pleasurable time in your life. It might be the day your son was born or the day you met your beloved. It might be a particularly exhilarating day you once had on the ski slopes or a wonderful night of dancing in Brazil. Whatever it is, if you can recapture the feeling of that experience, you can lift and transform your mood within seconds.

You can also become skilled at transforming the mood of your beloved, delighting them with treats you know they will love. A favorite story from one of my clients who works for a leading insurance provider involves a terrible day when she lost several major clients. You can imagine how she was feeling by the time she left the office that night and drove home.

However, when she walked into her home she discovered a note from her partner next to a bottle of French champagne. The note told her how much he loved her and invited her to get changed into something glamorous for a night of fine dining and dancing. It also informed her that a limousine would be arriving shortly to pick her up and to take her to the restaurant where he proposed marriage. In an instant her black mood was gone and she became a lover, setting aside the anger and distress she had been feeling.

Dare to Stand Apart

Once you know and accept that you are on a sacred mission, your perspective tends to change. Instead of feeling alone and vulnerable to the vicissitudes of life, you now have a partner who you can consult at any moment of the day or night.

How does it feel to know that you and your Soul are now life partners? Exciting? Reassuring? Nurturing? It is all this and much, much more. I consider this relationship with our Soul to be our primary life partnership. If this primary relationship is working, then everything else in our lives tends to be in harmony. Many people are looking for a Soul Mate—a romantic partner who will complete them and make them happy. In fact, we seldom find lasting happiness externally. The key to a Magnificent Life is discovering that the Soul Mate you seek is actually the one who resides within.

Once you have tidied up the relationship with your Soul, you might notice you are starting to attract the right sort of external relationships. After all, how will you be clear about the types of friendships you want or the attributes your Soul Mate should have if you do not know what makes you tick?

Your Magnificent Life

In reading this book, listening to the meditation, and doing the exercises, you are indicating that you may be willing to be passionate about your life and the things you want to achieve. You might recognize that this life that you have is not a dress rehearsal. Hopefully, you will choose to live your life with great energy, enthusiasm, flair, and passion. Perhaps you will discover that you are no longer prepared to play small to please others. Then you are prepared to commit to your own Magnificent Life.

At this stage you are probably feeling very challenged by the things that you feel are not working in your life. Your list may include such things as stress, poor health, unhappy relationships and lack of balance. What about the things you do want? Most people usually find it far more difficult to say what they do want, but it is an essential first step towards creating a Magnificent Life.

Oaths and Vows

What do I mean by committing to your life? The Hebrew Bible contains many stories of people making commitments to God that had life or death consequences. Genesis Chapter 22 tells us that Abraham was even prepared to sacrifice his beloved son Isaac to keep his commitment to God.

When making traditional oaths and vows, a petitioner often requested, "May God strike me dead if I do not keep my promise." Making a promise to God was an extremely serious undertaking in which the stakes were very high. Personal integrity and public reputation were on the line, not to mention the spiritual repercussions of death, disease, or pestilence that was believed to result from the failure to live up to one's commitments.

Commitment

There are many different types of commitments and various levels of committing that are not necessarily at the level of Abraham's. For instance, signing a legal contract to buy a house may feel like a greater obligation than signing up at the local gym.

The Oxford Dictionary defines commitment as *an engagement that restricts freedom of action*. So joining a sports team implies a social contract to the other members of that team. The would-be sportsperson doesn't sign any contract, but there is still an understood commitment to the team that he or she will turn up for games, practices, and other team meetings. If that social contract is not met, it will reflect badly on the person's reputation and trustworthiness. They may even forfeit their place.

Then there is commitment to your Soul, which involves the depth of your commitment to your own personal development. In order to bring about positive, lasting change in your life, it is necessary for your Soul to experience you as being serious about doing so. Each time you keep your word to yourself by doing what you need to do to achieve your goal, your relationship with your Soul is strengthened. You experience yourself as trustworthy and full of integrity.

Commitment On Behalf Of Others

While you can influence others, it seldom works to make a commitment on behalf of someone else. I have worked with people whose spouse or boss wanted them to quit drinking. They would turn up in my office for a counselling session and tell me their husband or wife had a problem because they were always nagging them about their alcohol consumption. If their partner would just accept their drinking, they argued, there would not be a problem. Likewise, I have had a diabetic client whose wife wanted him to take his insulin but he wouldn't, simply because he didn't want to be told what to do.

The person you have the most hope of changing is you, and your level of commitment to doing so is key to the level of success you will probably enjoy. To make a permanent and lasting change, this self-commitment has to be renewed every day until new habits, thoughts, and beliefs are formed. It is also important to realize that old habits don't go away, they remain beneath the surface waiting to be reactivated. So the alcoholic is still an alcoholic, even when dry. The gambler still wants to roll the dice, even when he puts new habits in place to minimize the possibility that he will.

Before designing and developing new habits, it is important to make a commitment to your Soul. Have you noticed that our western society tends to be commitment-phobic? We live in a time when everything is changing so fast that permanency is a concept that no longer seems to have much currency. Along with technology, even relationships have become disposable.

A Solemn Vow

Now, please consider making a commitment to your Soul. As we have seen, this is a solemn vow, not to be entered into lightly. Think of it as being as sacred and binding as a marriage. You are promising to love, honor and obey (or whatever words you prefer) your own inner spiritual guide.

What does that mean on a practical level? It means listening to your Soul every day by making quiet time to check in with yourself. It means finding out what you really want for your life and then pursuing it with vigor and integrity.

I suggest taking baby steps with this until the new habits find a solid foundation in your life. Start by committing to an ideal day for one day out of your week. Then do it with integrity and experience yourself as keeping your word. Next week, consider making the same commitment for two ideal days and so on.

For example, many years ago I made a sacred commitment to myself that I would honor my body every morning at 6am through an exercise program. I want to live to age 120 and I know I will need a strong body as a major ally to serve me in my later years. So, I started my fitness program gently, starting with simple stretching exercises for just a few minutes at a time. I gradually extended the time period and then the challenge of the actual exercises, until I felt ready to start a running schedule. Over the years, I have continued to modify my program to adapt to my changing needs; however, this habit and the honoring of the commitment remains a stable and important fixture in my life.

Sometimes other people in your life will not understand the decisions you make. New experiences can be both challenging and exhilarating at the same time. However, I can promise you this. As you move more and more into living a Magnificent Life of your own design, your Soul will also sing with the yes-ness of knowing you are doing what it takes to be who you came here to be.

Summary

In Chapter One we discussed the idea that you are more than just a body, a personality, and the roles you play. You are, in fact, a Soul having a human experience. As a unique, divinely created incarnate angel, you actually have a UPF that is the combination of all your special talents. Your Sacred Mission is the outworking of those talents in the world or, to quote Marianne Williamson again, it is the special way you can manifest the glory of God within you.

Now I am asking you to make a solemn commitment to Your Sacred Mission by asking your Soul to be your primary life partner.

Making Your Commitment

When you feel ready to do so, turn to the commitment sheet at the end of this chapter. Remember, this is just between you and your Soul. Allow yourself a quiet meditative space before writing anything down.

Exercise One

Preparation Meditation

Before making your commitment you might find a meditation useful. Here are some suggestions:

1. Put on comfortable, loose clothing.

2. If you choose, darken the room and light candles, oils or incense.

3. Turn off all phones and pagers. Make sure your colleagues or family know you are not to be disturbed for at least 60 minutes.

4. Find a comfortable position, either sitting with legs uncrossed on a chair or lying on the floor. (Don't do this if you think you might fall asleep).

5. You could listen to the guided meditation once more or simply close your eyes and focus on your breathing. One way to clear your mind is to imagine a black velvet curtain. In your mind's eye visualize standing in front of the curtain and pinning a piece of paper with the number 100 on the curtain. Look at the number 100 for five seconds and then take it down and replace it with 99. Keep doing this until your mind is free.

6. Once you are feeling completely relaxed, call in your Soul.

7. Imagine your Soul is sitting with you in your living room. You are communing like old friends. Feel what that feels like.

8. Now reach over and take your Soul's hand in yours. Tell him or her how happy you are to have him in your life. Tell him how you have missed him.

9. When you are ready, tell him you want him to be with you every step of the way from now on. Ask him to tell you what it is he really wants of you. Ask him to help. Stay with him for as long as you need.

10. When you are ready to come back, thank your Soul for coming to be with you and ask if you can make a date to talk again. State when you want to have this date (place and time).

11. Slowly return to the room, focusing on your breathing once more.

12. When you are ready, write your responses to the following exercises. If you have not yet completed your Sacred Mission statement, now is the time to do it.

My Sacred Commitment

I, _____, take you, my Soul, to be my primary life partner. I acknowledge that you give my life purpose, meaning and joy.

Having you in my life is important to me because

_____

_____

_____

I commit to checking in with you every day

at _____ for _____

and _____ for _____

and _____ for _____

I believe the rewards of going into partnership with you include

_____

_____

_____

I also acknowledge that as well as rewards there may be other consequences resulting from this partnership that may or may not be pleasurable. These could include

_____

_____

_____

The strength of my commitment is symbolized by

_____

_____

_____

Signed _____

Date _____

Symbolic Ritual or Ceremony

Soul commitments are as sacred as a marriage contract. Marking them with a special ceremony or ritual is important. It could be as simple as lighting a white candle or preparing a special meal. Some people buy themselves a ring or some jewelry as a physical reminder of the commitment. Take a few moments to decide what would work for you. Would you like witnesses or is this better as a private ceremony with your Soul? You decide. Write down what ritual you would like to perform to mark this occasion and either do it now or plan a date and time when it can be done.

3

The Magnificent Life

"The creation of something new is not accomplished by the intellect but by instinct acting from inner necessity. The creative mind plays with the objects it loves." Carl Jung

Do you remember the popular television program in the late 1960s called *Mission Impossible*? Every week a mysterious voice on a telephone would issue team leader Jim Phelps a seemingly impossible mission for him and his colleagues to perform. And, every week, despite the odds stacked against them, this team of brilliant operators and masters of disguise would prove their ability to rise above and master the impossible.

You could say that each week Jim Phelps and his colleagues became *Maniacs with a Mission*. The word maniac may have negative connotations of someone who displays obsessive behavior. However, the Oxford dictionary also describes a maniac as someone with extravagant enthusiasm. In this context, I'm referring to someone with passion.

If we use the *Mission Impossible* team as our model, we can say that they approached each new challenge with one-minded passion to find a way to accomplish the mission. If they had simply approached the challenge using orthodox methods of thinking, they would have concluded that the problems were indeed impossible and that they should just give up and go home. Instead, by single-mindedly applying creative problem-solving in conjunction with their individual and group resources and skills, they were able to design solutions that inspired the viewer with their ingenuity and resourcefulness.

I'd like to challenge you to become a *Maniac with a Mission* in your own life, which means becoming one-minded. Your mission, should you

45

decide to accept it, is to design a Magnificent Life for yourself, based on who you know yourself to be and how you want to express your own special creativity.

Before we can design a Magnificent Life, we need to get clear about those things for which we feel passionate. Sometimes we submerge who we are to put all our energy into our jobs or into pleasing others. Once we are in tune with our inner Soul Partner, it usually becomes more and more straightforward to discover those things that we love to do.

For instance, I know, without a shadow of a doubt, that I absolutely adore my wife and Soul Mate. No one ever has to convince me to be with her, and I love going for early morning walks with her. On the other hand, I can't imagine finding the energy or enthusiasm for going on a hunting trip, as this is something that simply doesn't appeal to me.

Likewise, I'm sure you have a list of things you love to do. Any day that contained one or more of these favorites would be memorable. Perhaps you love spending time in a garden, reading a book in front of an open fire, playing a game of tennis or having a round of golf. A day containing one or more of these activities would definitely be an enhanced day for you. Each of these pleasurable, Soul-enriching experiences is, in my terms, a 10. What do I mean by a 10?

10s

Tens are rewards for the Soul. They are **daily** Soul choices that make us feel glad to be alive—simple joys you can make happen every day. They are the fun, nurturing, and delightful treats that make any day worth living. Sometimes other people can also give us 10s. For instance, our children or partner might give us a cuddle and say, "I love you." Tens can also be spontaneous. Sunrises and sunsets happen every 12 hours and we have to seize the opportunity and notice them if they are to be a 10 on any particular day. The ideal is to have a 10/10 day by continuing to add 10s until you have a day that is so good it rates a top score.

Depending on your Unique Psychological Fingerprint, your list of 10s might include treats like having the whole family gather for Sunday lunch, or it might be the precious solitude you enjoy when you walk the dog each day, or the cuddles your son gives you at bedtime, or even the romantic dinner you plan with your beloved. Tens are ordinary, simple pleasures.

Once you bring your 10s to awareness, record them in your journal. In this way you may start to realize how wonderful your life really is and in those moments you may feel a sense of gratitude that you are alive. Imagine a day that is so wonderful that if you were to give it a score, it would be 10 out of 10. Now imagine a whole week of 10s—then a month. Wouldn't that be wonderful?

The 10s of Your Sub-Personalities

Go to Exercise Two at the end of this chapter. Without thinking too hard about it, start writing a list of your 10s. When the ideas are no longer flowing, start calling in your major sub-personalities and asking each of them to tell you his or her 10s. What about the mother in you? What does she enjoy? Perhaps she likes cuddles with her children or pets. Perhaps the woman in you likes some *me* time like a bath with candles. Or maybe the woman in you enjoys cooking for others.

What about the lover in you? Perhaps your list of lover 10s might include going out to dinner with a romantic partner, going dancing or writing poetry for that someone special in your life. What about your inner child? His or her 10s might include things like watching children's movies, singing karaoke or going skating. The magic of 10s is that we can have them, no matter how old we are, our gender or where we live in the world. Better yet, they never wear out. Each time they are experienced, they still seem wonderful.

Ask Other People What Their 10s Are

A good way to add to your own list of 10s is to ask others what would be on their list. Ask all the people you love. You might like to write down their answers so you know how to give these special people in your life treats in the future. Imagine how surprised and thrilled your partner would be if you planned a whole day of 10s for her. It might start with breakfast in bed then shopping at her favorite boutiques. You might even include a massage and facial and then conclude with a romantic, candlelit dinner at a restaurant you both enjoy. Think how you would totally amaze her with a whole day filled with treats.

In the same way, you could plan a day of 10s for your parents or children. You might even decide to have a day of 10s for your business partner or work colleagues. Think of how your special relationships might be enhanced if you looked at people and life in this way.

A day of 10s, whether for yourself or someone else, doesn't necessarily have to be expensive. Often it is simply about taking time out from your normal routine to have *me* time. Some people love starting their day with a jog or walk, others feel special if they start their day by cuddling their partner or children. Fresh flowers, aromatic candles, walking your dog, talking to a friend on the telephone, a swim in the ocean, a glass of fine wine with dinner—any of these can be 10s if they have the power to elevate a humdrum day into one that is magnificent.

Rules About 10s

There are some simple rules to keep in mind when designing your 10s. The first is that 10s can be enjoyed every day of your life and still bring you pleasure. If you love to arrange fresh flowers in your home then that is a joy that you could easily do every day and never tire. The second rule is that 10s cannot be dependent on someone else performing an action or task. For example, you can't decide that a 10 would be for your son to tell you he loves you. That could very well give you pleasure, but it is not something you can control. Instead your 10 might be telling him that you love him. Tens are things you can only give yourself or others.

Have you thought of more 10s to add to your list? Notice your body's responses as you write. Are you smiling? Do you feel happy just thinking about the small pleasures that enhance your life? Can you imagine enjoying them every day?

Having 10/10 Days

Decide that tomorrow will be your first 10 out of 10 or 10/10 day. Think about how you can add 10s into your schedule. Then make a commitment to giving yourself a whole day that is filled with 10s.

At regular intervals tomorrow, tune in with yourself. At 10am, 12 noon, 3pm and 5pm, ask, "What score would I give my day at this moment?" Then keep giving yourself more and more 10s from your list until it truly feels like a 10/10 day. Continue giving yourself 10/10 days until they become your normal experience of living. No matter how busy your life, always take time to stop and enjoy the beauty of a flower, to appreciate the gift of being healthy, to watch a sunrise or sunset, or to enjoy a kiss and cuddle with someone you love. Moments of awareness and appreciation like this are essential if you want to live a Magnificent Life.

25s

Twenty-fives are like that too. They give you the same pleasure as 10s, the difference is simply in the frequency. Twenty-fives are treats you can give yourself every two weeks or once a month and not get tired of them. They might be things like having a pedicure, going to the movies or taking your spouse or family out to dinner.

Perhaps you love catching up with friends for coffee, but you wouldn't want to do it any more frequently than once every two weeks because you might run out of things to say. Or, if your Toastmasters or Rotary group met every week you might find it too much of a commitment, whereas every two weeks is perfect.

You can enjoy frequent 10s and 25s because, by their very nature, they can become part of enriching your daily, weekly and monthly quality of life.

50s and 75s

Fifties and 75s are what I describe as intensely pleasurable, special experiences. Part of the enjoyment comes from the fact that you only do them once or twice a year because more frequently would lessen their impact and specialness.

If you and your partner had lunch in Paris for your anniversary, it would be a 50 because it is so special. If the two of you invited a group of friends along to join you for that special anniversary lunch, then the addition of the group of people that you love to spend time with would take the trip from a 50 to a 75. Get the idea?

At the end of this chapter you will have the opportunity to write some lists of 10s, 25s, 50s and 75s. You might also like to start some lists for the people you are closest to. For now, start thinking about the things you already have in place and what you would love to add to your life that would further enhance your zest for living. What about a trip on the Orient Express? Taking an Alaskan cruise? Going on safari?

100s

What about 100s? These are the big rewards for the Soul—the celebration that is extra special, mind-blowing and, tax-deductible. This could be the lunch in Paris where you invite your friends and colleagues to research an investment.

One of the far-reaching benefits from adopting 10s, 25s and 50s into your lifestyle is that—in addition to the pleasure these areas are likely to bring you personally—this pattern of being good to yourself will also have a positive impact on your productivity. Find that hard to believe? Well, think back to the last time you went on a short trip or just had a day off. Did you notice that when you returned to work your productivity increased significantly? Did your output also increase in the day or two before you left? That's because your Soul has been rewarded, and is now prepared to help you achieve and fund your life so that more rewards will follow. Certainly, I find that it's so much easier to stay single-minded and work-focused when I've planned treats and retreats for my Soul throughout each day, week and month.

Groups and Habits

Let's digress for a moment and discuss habits. We human beings are creatures of habit who often like to move in groups. These groups may be family based, employment based, or based around common spiritual beliefs or geographical settings that can influence our behavior, beliefs, attitudes, and perceptions. In our first few years of life, we develop the habits and attitudes of the dominant groups with which we associate. These include our family, church and educational institutions. Many people believe that these habits are God-given, that they are the right way to live. Actually, they are repetitive patterns of behavior that children copy from their parents, teachers and other dominant adults in order to survive and get approval.

Later, as we move into adolescence, our peer group exerts increasing influence, often causing us to conflict with the families into which we were born. The kinds of things that can change are language, manners, the way we take in information and the way we deal with anger.

Habits need to be seen in the context of the individual. For instance, the child living in a war zone may develop a habit of stealing food in order to survive. This cannot be regarded in the same way as the child growing up in a wealthy suburb who starts shoplifting because he is seeking adventure and attention. Context is very important.

At some point in our lives we become aware of obsolete habits that have become as outmoded as old furniture in a new home. Imagine you have just inherited a lot of money and you buy a wonderful mansion in a very exclusive area. If you move your old furniture into the new abode, it just doesn't look right.

Obsolete habits are like this. If you set a goal to run a marathon, suddenly your 10 cigarettes a day smoking habit does not serve what you now want to achieve. Likewise, if you desire that gorgeous new dress you saw in your favorite boutique and the dress is a size 10 and you are currently a size 14, then your nightly habit of eating ice cream and chocolate sauce for dessert may not be beneficial if your goal is to wear that dress when you go to the office party next month.

Does It Serve or Sabotage?

Once a habit pattern is established, we can follow it without thinking, thereby conserving our body's energy. This is biologically efficient. We can drive from the office to our home without needing to think too hard about it. As long as we still pay attention to the road ahead, this ability to get to our home each night without reading a map or asking for directions is energy efficient.

There are other habits that serve us that are necessary for our survival. Breathing is a repetitive action that is absolutely essential for life. However, if we developed a lung disorder and were hooked up to a breathing apparatus and had to push a button every few seconds in order to be able to breathe, it would be difficult to achieve much else in our day. Pushing the button would have to become a new habit if we wanted to survive. To learn this new habit we would have to focus on it and repeat it over and over until we could do it without conscious thought.

Think about the many habits you unconsciously perform every day. You may like to make a list. Breathing. Waking up. Boiling water for coffee. Showering. Brushing your teeth. Putting one sock on after the other. The list is endless.

Now make a list of the habits that no longer serve you. Such as talking to the office gossip when you know you should be contacting clients. What about the overworking that causes you to come home tired and stressed? How about not spending quality time with your family?

Are you spending hours each day talking over the fence to your neighbor? Or watching TV? Or sleeping because you don't know how to fill the hours of wakefulness? Do these habits serve the person you now choose to be or are they taking you away from things you would rather be doing?

Obsolete Habits

I once had a client who was a CEO of a national company who had moved to a new home and neighborhood. One night without thinking he drove to his old house by mistake. He thought he had arrived home and put the key in the lock. Of course it wouldn't work so he started pounding on the door and calling for his wife to let him in. The new owners woke up and called the police. When the police arrived everything was satisfactorily resolved. The new home/old home metaphor is quite an appropriate way of assessing obsolete habits.

The Enculturation Process

Imagine missionary parents have identical twins. The twins get separated and one grows up with a tribe in the jungle highlands of Papua, New Guinea, learning how to hunt and fish. The other one grows up with his parents in Cleveland, Ohio, going to school and church and learning how to be a model US citizen.

The twins are from exactly the same gene pool and yet grow into completely different people because of their enculturation processes. In other words, the groups they belong to have different value systems. For the child growing up in a Papua, New Guinea tribe, habits enabling survival and shelter are all important. He has to learn how to find a safe place to sleep at night and to feed himself by catching or trapping food.

The child growing up in prosperous Cleveland does not have to battle for daily survival. He has a roof over his head and food in his belly. The most important values he learns are things like respect for his parents and elders, manners and how to do well in school.

What often happens in adolescence—and middle age—is a questioning of this enculturation process. Until these major stages of development, the individual is swept along with the structures and habits he or she has been given by his or her dominant group. The upheavals of adolescence and middle age are part of a refining process. The individual decides, consciously or not, what habits from the original group habit pattern should be retained and then finds ways to personalize them.

Small and Tall Poppies

Now, I'd like to share with you some terms I learned in my early visits to Australia. I feel these terms are relevant to what I'm addressing in this book. To begin let me explain my understanding of the expression Small

Poppy. To be accepted in the Small Poppy culture, there is pressure to stay the same as everyone else. This is often reflected with sameness in dress, ornaments, speech, music and material goods. The need to belong to a group, gang or collective is a survival instinct that human beings have developed over time perhaps because it provided the greatest protection against predators and because we are social creatures. The Small Poppy looks outside himself to tell him what he should choose for his life. For many who are living the Small Poppy lifestyle it is preferable to live without the pressure of reaching the next stage of development or what is called Tall Poppy.

It seems to me that many people spend the 120 or so years they could have on this earth in cruise control. Too often they leave prematurely at age 70 or 80. Often people seek a life where they can feel comfortable and expend as little energy as possible. They get themselves a job and then develop habits around it that don't require too much thinking. They look to their work colleagues, neighbors and advertising in order to decide what they should want out of life. These are all Small Poppy behaviors.

The Tall Poppy is one who is able to look inside to find his/her direction. Their inner wisdom is sufficiently well developed to provide the guidance needed to achieve what they want in their life and how to live it.

Tall Poppies seek to unfold the fullness of who they truly are, while not being constrained by the expectations of other well-meaning people in their lives. Ideally, they decide what things they really love and choose to make a life of them—rather than live a life of accepting whatever comes their way.

On a regular basis, Tall Poppies review their life to ensure that their habits are working for them. When they find a habit that is obsolete—for example, smoking or not getting enough exercise—they take steps to change it. These people often work with a life and/or business coach. They are constantly focusing and refocusing on their goals and where they want to go in their life. They are in conscious connection with their Soul and use their Black Belt power to create their life. Tall Poppies seek to be who they are and are aligned with their destiny path. At first, it can be a lonely journey. They feel like they are standing apart from the group; however I encourage Tall Poppies to seek new friends and form their own communities where they are seen and appreciated for who they are. I call these *sacred communities*.

The first step to becoming a Tall Poppy is to work with your Soul to get clearer and clearer about who you are and what you want to create in your life. A primary tool for doing this is meditation. Meditation can encompass a whole range of forms, from sitting quietly for a time dedicated to communion with the Soul to bringing reverent attention to whatever you're doing, whether washing the dishes or walking around your garden—all the activities you can do to work with your Soul on a daily basis.

Big Rocks

And finally, there is another category of elements for a Magnificent Life that I would like to share. I call them Big Rocks. I was introduced to this concept many years ago at a conference where the speaker shared the following parable.

A Professor stood up in front of his class and placed a large punch bowl filled with fist-sized rocks on his desk. The rocks were stacked up like ice cream balls over the top of the bowl. He asked the class, "Is this bowl full?" They replied, "Yes."

The Professor then took a liter of pea gravel and added it to the bowl. He then shook the bowl, allowing the gravel to settle in the gaps between the rocks. The Professor then asked, "Now is the bowl full?" The class again responded that it was.

Then the Professor took a liter of sand, added it to the bowl and again gave it a shake. He asked, "Now is the bowl full?" This time the class responded with caution, many of the students said that they did not know any more.

Next, the Professor took a jug of water and added it to the bowl until it started to overflow. This time he asked, "What is the meaning of this story?" One pupil responded, "You can get more in than you thought." The Professor replied, "Yes, that's excellent. That's time management. We can fit more into our lives with good time management."

"However, that's not the interpretation I had in mind. The message I would like you to take away is that unless you get the Big Rocks of your life in first, you won't be able to fit them in. Your lives will fill up with the sand and pebbles, or what I call busy work so when it comes to that overseas trip you want to take you will never find the time."

To ensure you get in the Big Rocks of life it is important to plan ahead. We plan our holidays and adventures three years in advance so that we know they are in place. However, Big Rocks are not only the 75s or 100s of life—they can also include the rational, important decisions and actions we take as part of being prepared and secure. Big Rocks can include things that we don't necessarily like to do, such as having in-depth medical checkups, updating a will, and so on.

These important tasks may not be fun but they are necessary. They are about taking responsibility for our lives and those of our loved ones. For instance, I have my annual physical because as I get older, I want to be in the best of health—in a body that works. I believe in preventative medicine and so I want to ensure I know about any changes in my body's physiology. This is a rational decision for me rather than a passionate one.

Exercise One

10s

In the space below, write your list of 10s. Remember, 10s are the simple pleasures that you could happily have every day and never get tired of them, such as walking the dog, a great cup of coffee or a cuddle with your baby. Keep adding to your list as you discover more and more 10s in your life. How many can you give yourself today? What about tomorrow?

Exercise Two

Major Sub-Personality 10s

From the list below or from your own self-knowledge, choose 4 to 6 sub-personalities that are major ones for you. Write a list of 10s for each one. Salesperson, Manager, Yuppie, Minister, Planner, Business Person, Organizer, Fine Human Being, Wise Person, Mother, Father, Grandmother, Grandfather, Lover, Adventurer, Comedian, Traveler.

Exercise Three

25s, 50s, 75s and 100s

Write lists for each of these, referring back to this chapter if necessary. Each time you think of more, add them to your lists.

Exercise Four

Habits

Make lists of your own habits, those you have right now and those you want to have, using the following headings:

Survival

Unconscious

Obsolete

New

Exercise Five

Now, list five Big Rocks you'd like to achieve before you leave the planet— to ensure that you have lived a Magnificent Life.

4

Making Dreams Come True

*"Nothing has a stronger influence psychologically on
their environment and especially on their children
than the unlived life of the parent."* Carl Jung

The Ideas Stew

Are you someone who has lots of great ideas? They could be ideas about
business, things you would like to create or experiences you would like
to have before you die. Often these ideas just seem to come to you in
unexpected moments, when you're daydreaming or driving or even in the
shower. It is a bit like there is a stew of ideas floating around you.

Occasionally one of your ideas might be really ingenious and you
think—hey that just might work. Maybe you take action, but more likely,
as you get caught up in the hurly burly of day-to-day life, the idea recedes
to the back of your mind and you forget about it.

Months or even years later, you may have the experience that someone
else turned that ingenious idea of yours into a great success. It's not as if
they stole your idea because after all, it only existed in your mind. Even
more amazing, they may live thousands of miles away from you. So how
can it happen that two people who don't know each other can come up
with the same brilliant idea? The term Mass or Collective Consciousness
has been coined to describe this stew of ideas floating around us in space,
which we can all access.

The point is, once you have an idea you have a choice as to what you
do about it. You can be temporarily excited about it and then forget about
it or you can take it, put energy into it and make it happen. There is a sys-

tematic mind process that needs to occur if you want to cultivate your idea and make it a reality.

Dreams

Dreams are visions or images of possibilities that you can have—like ideas or thoughts, they are energy. Some dreams can manifest spontaneously as *grace* in our lives, whether through prayer, meditation or by accident. You may have experienced the sudden manifestation of a dream. Perhaps you were offered your dream job out of the blue or you walked into a room and there was the Soul Mate you had been dreaming about for years.

Then there are the dreams that must be actualized, such as climbing in the Himalayas. If you don't plan the trip, book it and prepare by getting fit and learning how to climb, a dream such as this is unlikely to spontaneously occur. If it did, and you had not prepared by building your stamina, it could quickly turn into a nightmare.

Like the ideas we discussed before that soon get forgotten, if dreams are not actualized, if they are not kept alive and nurtured, they can vanish. We have all had the experience with our nighttime dreams of one moment experiencing the images with crystal clarity and in the next moment, when we return to wakefulness, the dream evaporates like raindrops after a sun shower. Life dreams are the same.

The Role of Dreams in Our Lives

Daydreams and night dreams have several levels. On one level they represent unconscious manifestations of the Soul talking to us in symbolic language. These symbols can be interpreted, made sense of and integrated. Dream language can be the externalization of Soul fragments; that is, a code for the conscious mind to unravel. At times they can also be prophetic, foreshadowing future events, if we can correctly unravel the meaning of the symbolism.

In the Bible, Genesis, Chapter 41, Joseph was able to interpret the Pharaoh's dream of seven fat and seven lean cows and seven fat and seven withered sheaves of wheat as meaning seven years of prosperity and seven years of famine. This information allowed the Pharaoh to plan strategies to corner the commodities market of Egypt and greatly enhance his wealth.

On the level we are approaching here, we are taking the impression of a dream—as a complete entity—and moving it from being energy and an image to becoming a concrete reality. If we dream of building a home and decide to make that dream a reality, we begin by buying the land. Then we work with professionals such as architects, bank managers, local government officials and craftsmen, who act like midwives, helping us to realize our dream.

Here we are taking the dream from the mental to the material world. If our Soul Partner has objections, it will make things happen that will sabotage the process. Let's say we decide to prospect for customers who will help us pay for our new home. Instead of prospecting we read newspapers, do busy work, have coffee and engage in activities that are self defeating. This is our Soul Partner's way of telling us that it has not yet bought into the actualization of the dream for a new home.

It is possible to find a way to discover our Soul's objection. Sometimes, even after much negotiation, our Soul's answer is still no. I have had such experiences in my own life. In 1978 I was single and looking to buy a home in Phoenix. I had the money and I found eight suitable properties. I put each of them under contract in the appropriate way. Over the next few weeks one burnt down, one was taken off the market, the owner of another raised the price while we were negotiating, the owner of another died and the house went into the estate. Needless to say, I didn't get my home. I went to Brugh Joy, my outer teacher and he reminded me by saying, "I guess it's not time for you to settle into your own home." Two years later I found and easily purchased a home which turned out to be perfect for me. It seems 1980 was the time for me to own a home, not 1978.

Spontaneous or Actualized

What makes some dreams take root and germinate while others are like scattered seeds that fall on barren ground? Imagine two young boys dreaming of swimming in the Olympics one day. Ten years later one of them makes it and the other one doesn't. Let's examine the possible reasons why.

It may be that the young boy who makes it onto the Olympic Team saw his destiny in a vision and then aligned with it—effectively claiming his intuitive knowing that this was what he had been born to do. The Tall Poppy nature in him—that wild, regal spirit—then rose to the challenge by taking the dream and clarifying it into an action plan. Then, day-after-day, he did whatever he had committed to in the action plan. For instance, he may have risen every morning at 4am to go to the pool to practice. He might have curtailed social activities in order to get to bed early each night so he could make this early start. In this way he actualized his dream.

On the other hand, the second boy may have had the same dream about how wonderful standing on the dais wearing the gold medal would be and did nothing about it. For him the dream remained as hazy and unformed as the dream you struggle to remember once you open your eyes in the morning. In the case of the second boy, the passion or desire to swim in the Olympics was not strong enough to propel him into action.

This is what I refer to as a spontaneous approach to dreams. It is like going to a movie or the theater. The dreams become exciting entertainment, providing some light relief and distraction from the humdrum reality of life, but they don't turn into reality.

The Impossible Dream

What about dreams that seem impossible because there is some aspect to them that cannot be controlled? For example, you may have dreamed your entire life of having children some day. As an adult you then discover that you are infertile.

With that discovery do you have to give up your dream? I don't believe so. Your choices are then more limited but there are still some courses of action available to you. Depending on your cultural context, you might consider in vitro fertilization or adoption.

Recently, I worked with a client who had cancer. Because he and his wife desired a family he had had his sperm frozen before undergoing radiotherapy treatments. Happily, his wife had conceived and they eagerly awaited the birth of their baby. They had taken what appeared to have been an impossible dream because of his poor health, and made it possible.

Cultural or Family Dreams

Sometimes we inherit or take on the dreams or expectations of others. For instance, it is often the case with immigrant families that the parents will work very hard and make sacrifices in order for the children to get a good education in their new homeland. The hope is that with an education they will secure a good career and be able to take care of the extended family.

There may also be cultural dreams or expectations. In Italy, among devout Catholics, there is prestige for the family if one of the sons goes into the priesthood or a daughter becomes a nun.

In my family history, my maternal grandmother had a dream in 1917 to get her family out of the Soviet Union to the safety of a new life in America. Even though she was not in good health and, in fact, died shortly after the family arrived in the United States, her dream kept the family going. Through six years of hardship and danger the family trekked across Russia, Poland and Germany, using jewels sewn into clothing to bribe the border guards. Thanks to the strength of my grandmother's vision, her three daughters survived to enjoy lives quite different from the ones they might have had in Communist Russia.

Unlived Dreams

Sometimes children take on the secondhand dreams of their parents. As stated at the beginning of the chapter, Carl Jung said, "Nothing has a stronger influence psychologically on their environment and especially on their children than the unlived life of the parent."

If the parent aspired to be a great musician or famous actor and did not achieve his or her dream, this can become an expectation on the child. The stereotypical stage mother who obsessively pushes her child to perform may be using her daughter to fulfill her own unlived dream of stardom. Family tradition can also influence a child's choice of career path. In professions such as law, medicine and politics it is quite common to find two or three generations of the same family where children have followed in parental footsteps.

Personal Dreams

When you live in harmony with your Soul Partner and experience a Magnificent Life filled with 10s, 25s, 50s and so on, you may find you become very attuned in discerning whether or not a dream is yours or someone else's.

I'd like you now to tune into a dream you have as I share with you one way in which you can make this dream come true. This systematic process is a way to actualize your dreams. I call this technique the **Eight Point Plan** and the key elements of the plan are:

1. Goal
2. Due Diligence
3. Commitment
4. Detailed Action Plan and Timeline
5. Mooring Lines
6. Do It
7. Celebrate
8. Review

Before we continue, let's take a moment to define some terms.

Goal

A goal is a bridge connecting a dream from NOW until its FULFILLMENT. Commitments are the stepping-stones on the bridge that pave our way to the dream-goal fulfillment in the material world. Writing a dream into a definite goal moves it closer to actualization by the very act of taking responsibility for it.

Commitment

A commitment is a tangible behavioral step towards achieving a goal that is completely within our own personal power and is not dependent on anyone else or external forces. A commitment is an action that we entrust ourselves to do, with an obligation that is as powerful as making an oath.

I might state my commitment like this: *I solemnly swear to my Soul that together we, as a partnership, will do the actions outlined in this Eight Point Plan to the full extent of my power and with the help of whomever I need.*

The world and life provide opportunity. We can say yes or no to those opportunities and have control of the responses we make to the choices offered in our life. The choices may come from a dream inside us or may come from outside challenges. If we plan a trip to Sri Lanka and it is devastated by a tsunami the week before we plan to go, then we postpone the trip until the time is right. We do not have control over the weather patterns.

Rewards and Non-Rewards

People set goals all the time, work towards them for a few weeks and then life gets busy or other things get in the way and somehow the goal—and the oath status of the original commitment—get buried, reprioritized or perhaps forgotten. That is why I believe we need to design some consequences, what I call non-rewards, for when we waver, postpone or lapse from our oath to Soul Partner.

Often the TV sitcom that grabs our attention is not part of a Soul Contract but serves as an avoidance of a commitment. The purpose of non-rewards is really to take personal oaths as seriously as one we might make to another person in a legally binding agreement. Rewards are designed to help us celebrate the fact that we have honored a commitment to ourselves.

Rewards and non-rewards work best when they are attached to individual commitments designed to achieve a goal.

Mooring Lines

Mooring lines are like the ropes that keep a boat tied to its mooring. In terms of our lives, they are any obstacles that appear to be stopping us or making it difficult for us to complete our plan and journey. The mooring lines may be physical, such as a blizzard or a broken ankle. Or, they may be psychological, "I'm too busy at work to go."

Eight Point Plan Example

Life on purpose requires planning. Life by accident doesn't. Follow the example given here and then in Exercise One, use the Eight Point Plan format to take a current dream of yours and turn it into an action plan.

Let's say the dream is to climb Mt. Kilimanjaro in Kenya. While we stay in a dream state thinking, "One day I'll climb Mt. Kilimanjaro," we maintain ourselves in a state of limbo and accept what comes to us in life. If we get to the end of our days and we still haven't climbed the mountain we might say, "Oh well, it just wasn't meant to be."

Making an Eight Point Plan moves it into our conscious awareness as an achievable goal. We then put the actions and strategies in place to actualize it.

Dream—To climb Mt. Kilimanjaro

Eight Point Plan—To climb Mt. Kilimanjaro in June next year

1. What do I want?—To climb Mt. Kilimanjaro, with my friends Rob and Chris, in June next year and to have done sufficient training to make the climb in a healthy and enjoyable way.

2. Due diligence—Have a comprehensive medical examination, acquire quotes for air fare and accommodations, consult with a personal trainer on fitness and stamina levels required, research and source altitude training, get quotes on the necessary equipment, and review insurances, my will and the family financial requirements for the time I will be away.

3. What is my commitment?—I commit to completing each of the actions in my plan with all my heart, soul and mind. The reward I give myself for achieving it is two days in a luxurious spa after the climb. The consequence or non-reward of deciding to pull out of the trip will be that I burn the non-refundable air ticket in front of Rob and Chris.

4. My detailed action plan and timeline—
  • Today—get my personal assistant to book me for a medical.
  • Tonight—plan the trip with Rob and Chris.
  • Tomorrow—hire a personal trainer.

- Work out three times a week with my trainer.
- Go to an Indoor Mountain Climbing course every Wednesday night.
- September—book trip and buy travel insurance.
- October—research altitude sickness.
- October—buy my equipment.
- December—trekking during Christmas vacation with my pack.
- January—talk to my accountant.
- April—get shots.
- April—have another medical exam.
- June 1—we're off!

5. Mooring lines I might use and solutions I might apply—

(a) Procrastination—I might put off starting my fitness program or I might start with gusto and then lose enthusiasm. To get around this I'm going to ask my fitness trainer to charge me double for any appointment I cancel. I'm also going to stay connected to my goal by reading this plan at the start of each day. I will also watch videos of climbs other people have done on the mountain. I will meet with Rob and Chris every two weeks to talk about our trip.

(b) Sickness or Injury—I've noticed that in the past when I've planned a big adventure such as this, I've become ill and had to pull out at the last minute. Strategies I can put in place to avoid this include looking after myself by eating well, getting enough rest and saying affirmations each day that I am healthy, fit and well. To avoid injury I will warm up properly before I start each training session and I will say affirmations each day that I am surefooted as a goat.

6. Do it!—I've completed intensive training, had my medical exams and we leave next week.

7. Celebrate—Rob, Chris, and I are going to have a huge party to celebrate our success when we get home. The venue is booked and we've already told all our friends and family.

8. Review—Upon returning home and when I'm down from my high, I'll review how I would do this better next time. Then I'll write my Eight Point Plan for the next goal I want to achieve.

Peer Partners

One thing I discovered when I began working on my Eight Point Plan was that it is especially helpful to have someone on my side, who will keep me on track—someone I can be accountable to. Someone who will also ensure that when I meet my commitments, I reward myself, and if I don't meet them, he will make sure I pay the consequences.

I call this kind of relationship a Peer Partnership. I recommend that you consider seeking a peer partner who is at your level—someone whom you respect and feel you can trust. When you choose to work with a peer partner, you are making a commitment to be accountable to them and to hold them accountable. You give each other permission to hold your feet to the fire to ensure that you both really achieve what you set out to do.

If you're contemplating something like the Mt. Kilimanjaro climb, you might want to approach one of your fellow climbers to be your peer partner during the challenging preparation period. After all, they want to go on the trip too and will have to do similar training in order to get there.

Whether your goals are professional or personal, I suggest you have weekly reviews with your peer partner. In this relationship, you both have no other agenda than to ensure you're still doing what you are undertaking to do. If mooring lines have snared you, then a peer partner is an ideal sounding board for discussing what happened, how you dealt with it this time, and how you might deal with a similar situation in the future.

Your sessions can be face-to-face or on the phone, and it's a good idea to schedule your reviews several weeks in advance at an agreed time so there's no excuse for not meeting. It's important that you get into the habit of updating each other by fax or email. Your peer partnership may well become one of the most important business or personal development relationships in your life.

When you decide to set up a peer partnership arrangement with someone, there is a standard protocol to follow in the first meeting that you can also use as an agenda for future meetings. Share with your partner, the following:

1. Your business and personal goals.

2. A maximum of three commitments that you are ready to make as steps towards achieving your goals.

3. The rewards and consequences you are setting around the achievement or nonachievement of each commitment, and enlist support in some way to ensure that these are observed.

4. The mooring lines that are likely to emerge and could get in the way as you start to work on your commitments. What are the usual ways you sabotage your own success?

5. A list of 10 or more of your 10s as well as potential 100s and Big Rocks.

6. Review the notes that you've each taken on the other's goals, commitments and concerns and ask each other, "Is there anything I've missed, anything else I should know?"

7. The best time and method for accounting to each other—and then do it!

The goal of a peer partnership is not to be nice, but rather to help each other achieve business and personal goals. Often you'll find your peer partner will tell you things that your family and friends would love to tell you but don't. Your family doesn't want to say anything even if they see your money or reputation going down the drain.

In a peer partnership you each have the mandate to be tough and confront each other's inconsistencies if and when necessary. This is a valuable gift of honesty and tough love. It can often mean the difference between just cruising and letting things slip, or stopping, taking stock of what's really happening (or not happening), and then taking the appropriate action to correct your course. I feel immense gratitude to the people in my life who have taken the time to be peer partners to me at critical times on my own journey.

Exercise One

The Eight Point Plan

Choose a dream that you would love to fulfill. Using the Eight Point Plan format, take your dream and turn it into an action plan. Make sure you complete every part, including rewards, non-rewards and mooring lines.

Exercise Two

My Ideal Peer Partner

1. Make a list of attributes and qualities you would like in a peer partner.

_____

_____

_____

2. Make another list of things to avoid in a peer partner.

_____

_____

_____

3. Make a short list of people you might ask to partner with you.

_____

_____

_____

4. Approach the person you would most like to work with, explain the concept to them and arrange your first meeting.

5. My first meeting with my peer partner is _____

6. I would like to discuss

_____

_____

_____

_____

Exercise Three

Mooring Lines

1. Fill in the following questionnaire, being honest with yourself about past behavior and experiences. You may like to share it with your Peer Partner.

2. Mooring lines I have used to prevent myself from making my dreams come true.

_____

_____

_____

_____

3. Mooring lines I use to prevent myself having a 10/10 day, every day.

_____

_____

_____

_____

4. Mooring lines I have called upon to help me sabotage my business.

_____

_____

_____

_____

5. If I were not afraid of _____

_____

I would

_____

_____

_____

_____

5

Channels of Consciousness

"We cannot change anything unless we accept it.
Condemnation does not liberate, it oppresses." Carl Jung

Your Inner TV

In Chapter Four we worked through the process of taking a dream—which is blurry and unfocused—and turning it into an achievable goal through the appropriate commitments and attention to mooring lines that might get in the way. This is a little like the process of tuning your television set to eradicate the horizontal lines or focusing the lens on a camera to give a clearer image. Once we get specific about a goal, we can start visualizing how it would be to have it in our lives. This in turn provides the energy or fuel for us to take the actions and create the habits necessary in order to manifest the goal.

In this chapter we are going to take the analogy of the television set even further. I believe that our mind is like a multidimensional television set with potentially a million different channels that we can access—although most of us are still only using one, two or three of the million channels available. Just think about that for a moment—a million channels available to you. If you could learn to use more and more of these channels, what difference might that make to your life?

One-Mindedness

One way it might make a difference is by giving you the freedom to separate out the various facets of your life and place them on their own channel. If you had a channel for eating, another for sleeping, another for work, yet another for driving and so on, this would potentially give you the ability to be fully focused on the task at hand, whatever it is, instead of juggling several activities at once. I call this One-Mindedness.

Awareness Continuum

The Awareness Continuum is the flow of awareness. Like a flowing river, our awareness comes to us in a steady stream. Every three seconds or so, we become aware of something new. Right now I am aware of my fingers tapping the keyboard, now I am aware of the hum of my computer, now I am aware of the sound of a bird singing outside my window and so on. The foreground of my awareness is what I'm paying attention to in the moment and this is an organic process. When I tap into this flow of awareness, I am tapping into the real me.

At any time, we can override this flow of awareness with our rational mind. Perhaps we suddenly remember that our taxes are due next week and we have to get the information ready for our accountant. We can then choose to move our awareness to worrying about how we are going to get our taxes done in time or we can stay with what we are aware of right now.

The flow of awareness can be diverted by external conditions. Perhaps the telephone rings and I choose to answer it. Talking to the person on the other end of the phone then diverts my flow of awareness for the next few minutes. The advertising industry and the media are experts at grabbing our flow of awareness. Distracting or ambiguous headlines; colorful, in-your-face slogans; sound bytes; and visuals—all of these are designed to grab our flow of awareness so we will buy whatever is being touted. By becoming conscious of our present flow of awareness we can decide whether or not we choose to be distracted or diverted.

Background

Background is everything I am and everything I have ever experienced, as well as my response to my life experiences. It is my memories, hopes, dreams, beliefs, life experience, friends, the languages I speak, my education, travels and so on. At any given moment I have billions of bits of data stored in my bio-computer to call upon. Background is part of the Awareness Continuum. I could be thinking about my taxes, then thinking about what I'm having for dinner tonight and then I suddenly remember a wonderful meal I had in Italy 10 years ago.

In computer jargon, background is the equivalent of storing this information—and our response to it—on the hard drive of our mind. If I had been beaten as a child, I could use this information to become a bullying father or a loving father.

In the amazing bio-computer that is our brain, we have stored data going back to our birth and even to past lives. This data can be retrieved when required, just like finding an old file stored in the archives of your computer. The trick is to know when to be fully present to the task at hand and when it is appropriate to call upon stored data because it may offer some guidance or direction to your present situation.

Think of it this way. Without the ability to shift our awareness on the Awareness Continuum at will, we would be like computers with too many files open at once, which may slow down our ability to successfully complete the task at hand. If you are at work and your intention is to engage in producing income, then it is a distraction and inappropriate for you to be daydreaming about your tenth birthday party and how your mother made all your favorite treats, including chocolate cake. Either your soul is in rebellion or you simply need to bring your awareness to what sub-personalities are running you at the moment and what might be more appropriate to your goal of making a good living.

However, there are times when retrieval is very appropriate. If you are busily working away at your office and you suddenly realize you can't find the special pen your spouse gave you for your birthday, then an ability to mentally retrace your actions and where you've been that morning with your pen can help you retrieve that data. You remember that you had it in your pocket and then your son wanted some help with a problem for school so you took your pen from your pocket and showed him how to complete the math problem. While you were talking to him, you placed the pen on the kitchen table beside you and then you forgot to put it back in your pocket. Problem solved, you can now get back to the task at hand.

Channel Surfing

If most of us are only operating on one, two or three channels, it means all the things we could focus on are bombarding us simultaneously. Things can then become superimposed and our ability to concentrate becomes reduced. We jump from activity to activity; we start making a sandwich and then decide to water the houseplants. Halfway through that, we see that the garbage needs taking out, so we stop watering in order to put out the garbage receptacles. We are no longer in flow; instead we lurch from one half-completed task to another.

This is a bit like going channel surfing when you watch television. While channel surfing you might get snippets of the news, tennis match, police drama, sitcom, lifestyle show or documentary. You would be receiving image after image, many of which would have little or no relationship to the one that preceded it. If you kept this up for several hours, never stopping on one channel for longer than a few minutes, you would soon feel bombarded, confused and disoriented. Superimposing is like going into a store that sells television sets and seeing 50 TVs, all on different channels blaring forth. It can be absolutely overwhelming.

And yet, this is exactly the way most of us live our lives. Imagine this scenario. You've had a busy day at work and you feel tired. As you drive home, a client calls on your cell phone and you know this is crunch time to do a prospective deal. While you are speaking, the phone is simultaneously beeping as it registers text messages and emails as they are received. At the same time as your phone is beeping, your eyes are receiving images and impressions about the traffic and, in response to this information, your hands and feet are taking actions such as changing gear, braking and turning the steering wheel. Then your stomach growls, reminding you how hungry you are because you didn't stop for lunch today. You continue talking to your client, all the time wondering what to have for dinner. You mentally run through what food is in the house and realize that the choice is limited to last night's chicken leftovers unless you want to stop at the store on the way home. Suddenly the guy in the next lane cuts in front of you and you have seconds to react or you will hit him.

Sound familiar? This is just one example from a day that is probably crowded with such experiences. Is it any wonder many people feel stressed out with the constant juggling of all these competing thoughts and stimuli? None of the activities in our example are receiving the One-Mindedness they deserve. If you have an accident or the deal goes bad, you might get cranky and say it was a bad day but, in actual fact, it was your own channel surfing that created the stress.

Your Curriculum If You Accept It

The day—stressful or stress-free—is what happened. As I see it, your curriculum is sent by the Creator. Your challenge, your opportunity and your choice, is what you do with the day presented to you. This is where you exert your skills, training and power.

Your response will depend on your openness and personal life experience, as well as what you have integrated into your life path up to this moment in time. It will include your beliefs and your life experiences. A **Black Belt of the Mind** is usually able to turn any life experience into a 10 out of 10 experience, using his or her available skills.

The shift here is a life posture that sees everything that happens to us or that we create as an opportunity to say yes—to the challenges and gifts that life brings. I have learned most from the unique experiences in my life that were not slam-dunk successes. Rather, they were often things that I would have preferred not to have to deal with, yet they were the experiences that helped me grow.

When we see each day as a series of opportunities and challenges (the adventure of life itself), our choice then is to follow our plan and master the challenge at hand so it becomes a 10/10 for us. While we do not have control over much that befalls us, we do have total control of our responses. We can train ourselves on how we respond to life's challenges. I grew up in a tough neighborhood, so I had to develop the skills to survive in such an environment. The curriculum presented to us on a daily basis becomes our gift. As with the Bible story in the book of Jonah, often called the Reluctant Prophet, we learn that we cannot really say "no" to our curriculum because when we do, the challenges will pursue us until we face them.

Multitasking in Sequence

One-Mindedness is about being fully present in the moment. If you think back to times when you have achieved your best results—results that absolutely astounded you, you will see that you were giving whatever activity you were engaged in your undivided attention. Human beings function best if they have just one thing at a time in their focus. This does not mean that you should not multitask. What I am suggesting is that the most efficient form of multitasking is to deal with each separate task in sequence.

If you are in the middle of an important phone call and another call comes in, it is not efficient or respectful of the person with whom you are speaking to put them on hold while you take the other call. Multitasking in sequence could involve having your personal assistant take your other calls while you are on the phone. Then you could systematically return them once you are finished with the first conversation. Or, you could simply ensure that you have a good voice messaging system to capture the messages for your later attention.

With the advent of new technology such as the Internet, cell phones, and Palm Pilots, we have the ability to communicate very quickly. We can also juggle several different tasks at once. We could be answering emails as we speak on our hands-free phone. We have been taught that such doubling up of activities is saving time; however, our focus and our effectiveness is greatly reduced. One of the reasons for this is that it is easier to maintain a relaxed approach if dealing with one thing at a time. A relaxed state of mind is the optimum state for creative problem-solving. The next chapter discusses the importance of relaxation and offers some tips and techniques to reduce stress.

Remember our earlier example of driving home and having our cell phone ring? In that situation we have to choose whether or not to stay with the driving continuum or pull over to the curb and switch to a deal-making flow. Our decision will be influenced by whatever sub-personalities are present in that moment. If the spouse and father sub-personalities are the dominant ones during the drive home, then we will probably choose to return the call later so we can continue our homeward journey. If the negotiator and deal closer are dominant, we will probably take the call. Whatever the decision, it is best not to run several rivers of awareness at the one time because this divides our life force and creates a feeling of internal conflict.

Where Did You Go?

There is another very good reason why juggling several activities does not support successful communication and that is, people can feel it if your energy is retracted or fragmented. Let me explain what I mean by this. I have a client who is an American Express Financial Planner. One day I was speaking with him on the phone and my wife came into the room to wave goodbye before going off to her appointment. No words were spoken between us; I simply waved back to her and smiled. My client, who is very sensitive, immediately felt my energy shift and asked, "Where did you go? What just happened?" He was expressing a sense of mild rejection and hurt feelings at a time when he was baring his soul to me. This is similar to how your partner or child might feel if they are telling you something that happened to them that day and you pick up the newspaper and start reading or your cell phone rings and you answer it.

Respecting Others

If you are speaking with someone over the phone and, at the same time, you are answering your emails and checking your calendar—the person you are talking to may indeed feel that you are not really paying attention to him. He may experience that without even consciously expressing it and may feel you are not respecting him. He may even experience a mild sense of rejection. That experience alone might convince him that you are not the person with whom he wants to do business. If you are speaking to your beloved or child, they may feel hurt that you do not have time to really hear what they want to say to you. If these feelings accumulate over time and are reinforced by repeated behavior, it is likely to have a negative impact on your relationships.

Know What Channel You're On

Using our earlier example of driving home and doing a business deal at the same time, how might you have managed that situation more effectively with the one channel technique? It's important to decide what channel you want to be on. Is it more important to get home alive or to do the deal? If you choose the deal, please pull over to the curb and do it. Statistics show most accidents happen within a five-mile radius of home, because we know the roads so well we think we don't have to concentrate.

Technology such as cell phones and pagers can be distracting at the moment we should be exercising greater caution. According to Harvard University's Center for Risk Analysis, it is estimated that in 2003 over 1.5 million car accidents in the United States involved cell phone usage, with 2,600 fatalities and 330,000 reportable injuries.

The most important thing when driving an automobile is to be fully on the driving channel, focusing on the traffic and being alert to potential dangers. Ideally, we should not be speaking on our cell phones. When I return to New Zealand, where cars travel on the left-hand side of the road, I have to be very careful that I am fully on the correct channel when driving. Once, when I was tired and there were no other cars on the road, I strayed to the wrong side. Fortunately someone was in the car with me and pointed out my error. Although I am perfectly comfortable driving in either place, this is an example of what happens when I'm not fully on the channel. I have now developed a channel for driving in Australasia and another for driving in the United States.

The Dollar-Productive Business Channel

Channel 37 is the channel I refer to as the Business Channel. Optimum results in business come from being totally focused on Channel 37 while at work—which means doing only those activities that will produce income. I call these activities Dollar-Productive. Ideal sub-personalities for Dollar-Productive behavior would include the salesperson, the negotiator, the person of integrity and the astute business person. While on the business channel, it's important to avoid the sub-personalities that are not conducive to dollar productivity, such as the Distracter, the Victim, the Flirt and so on.

Let's take our earlier example of the deal-making or deal-breaking phone call with your client. Imagine you have arrived at your office. You know you have to call your client and close the deal; and you are still thinking about your sick daughter who is in bed with the flu and how tired your wife is after being up all night. Part of your focus is still on the Family Channel. How do you put yourself totally on the Business Channel and make the call with total One-Mindedness?

Getting On the Channel

Let me describe a process that seems to work for many of my clients. To begin, you have made the decision to be Dollar-Productive at this time, rather than a family caregiver and nurturer at home. Now your behavior needs to support that decision. If you know you will not be able to do Dollar-Productive activities because you are worrying about your family, you might make a call home to your wife to ensure that she and your daughter are both all right and that there is nothing more you can do.

That dealt with, it is time to bring your focus onto the Business Channel. The next thing you might do is ensure that you will not be disturbed. To achieve this you might adopt strategies such as asking your assistant to take all calls. You might close the door to your office. You might even put your telephone headset on so that anyone looking in will think you are already on the phone.

Fully Present

You have now controlled your environment as much as you can. In the process of ensuring privacy, you are also assisting that shift of your mind to be more fully present on Dollar-Productive business. So, what's next? To get your mind off your previously compelling family situation and onto the deal at hand, take a few minutes to sit comfortably and take some deep breaths, allowing the oxygen to travel to every cell in your body. Ask yourself, on a scale of 1 to 10, how present am I right now? Keep taking deep breaths and consciously letting go, until your score reaches a 9 or 10.

Once you are feeling totally present, I would suggest visualizing a time when you successfully closed a deal or when you provided exceptional service to a customer. You might recall that feeling of exuberance you had when the client said, "Yes, let's do it." Or, "Thank you so much." If you can, remember where you were at the time, what you were wearing, or what the client was wearing. What were the words you used and how did he respond? How did it feel when he said yes? What else do you remember about this particular situation? Recall as many specific details as you can and run the tape in your head. Most importantly, allow yourself to feel that feeling of success and celebration that came with the knowledge that you made the deal or exceeded your customer's expectations. This technique of mood switching using active visualization is called the Inner Movie Theater.

In our immediate context of closing the deal or being of real service, the important point to remember is that you can consciously take yourself to a memory that might assist the current situation. Altering your mood in this way not only allows you to focus better, it may also re-energize you when you're feeling tired and boost your confidence in your own abilities.

Call in Your Sub-Personalities

Next, consciously call in a selection of your sub-personalities that are experts in doing business. For instance, the Dealmaker, Negotiator and Tactician might all have some useful insights and knowledge for you to draw upon.

This is also the time to make sure that any inappropriate sub-personalities, such as the Child ("Aren't I cute?") or the Victim ("I couldn't help it, I did my best. You owe it to me!") or the Family Nurturer ("I wonder how my women are doing at home?") are not on the channel. You do not want to jeopardize your negotiations by saying or doing anything that might weaken your position.

100% in Charge

It is important to note at this point that, barring medical catastrophe, you are 100% in charge of this ability to call in sub-personalities to the foreground or relegate them to the background when your skills are developed and used regularly. Practice, as with most things, is the key.

Getting onto the Right Channel

So, how do you do this? For me, it is about psyching myself into the next external activity by preparing the inner me. This is what an athlete does when preparing for a race and the same principles can be applied to any activity.

In my capacity as a Rabbi, I used to prepare students for their Bar/Bat Mitzvah. These young people came to me nervous and concerned at the prospect of performing the ceremony in front of all their relatives and family friends. Much effort in their young lives had been leading up to this moment and they were often filled with fears that they would blank out, panic or embarrass themselves on such an important day. What if they looked at their mother and suddenly forgot every word they were supposed to say? Or worse, what if their younger sister made a funny face at them and they suddenly burst out laughing?

Together, the students and I created a channel called Channel Bar Mitzvah. I taught them how to stay on that channel, no matter what. I had them practice while the other students tried to distract them by calling out, whistling and jeering—even throwing spitballs. You guessed it, a year later when they had to stand up in front of 300 people, the young people performed amazingly well, seldom permitting anything to take away their focus.

Inner Movie Theater

In order to get the students onto the Bar Mitzvah Channel, we made use of a technique I call the Inner Movie Theater.

In unusual situations we can sometimes feel stressed because we are not sure what sub-personalities to call in and how to react to unfamiliar circumstances. Unconsciously we can move into feeling stressed. By using the Inner Movie Theater technique you can play the appropriate movie prior to an activity to help psych yourself into it.

In my example of the students learning how to perform their Bar Mitzvahs, we had to create positive images into which they could enter, so they could relax and feel confident about their ability to perform. Each student created an Inner Movie of what the occasion would look and feel like at its best. They imagined the synagogue where they would present, what they would wear, who else was present, what they could hear, smell, see, touch and feel. They then imagined their elation on successfully completing the ceremony and being congratulated by family and friends.

By creating tapes and gathering memories in a journal of beneficial experiences, you catalogue them for use in the future. This assists in helping you change your state of consciousness and move quickly from channel to channel without stress. You will have an opportunity in Exercise Two at the end of this chapter to create some tapes for your own Inner Movie Theater. For now, you might like to start thinking about and cataloguing the moments that stand out in your life as the most moving, impactful, happy and joyful.

Psyching Your Self for the Challenge at Hand

Using a tape recorder, visualize and record a very successful business deal that you closed. Remember every aspect of that day. Where were you? What were you wearing? What could you see around you while you were performing so well? What, if anything, could you smell? What could you hear? How did your own voice sound? What were you feeling?

Perhaps the exceptional business deal took place at a restaurant over lunch. Remember exactly what the restaurant, your table, your client and your meal looked like. Can you recall the dessert that you ate that day? Can you remember the color of your tie? The color of his shirt? The perfume of the flowers on the table? The view from the restaurant window?

Now focus on how you felt at that meeting. Did it feel as if everything was going your way and you knew exactly the right things to say at exactly the right time? How did it feel when the client said yes? How did it feel when you shook hands?

As you describe and record the moment of success, the sub-personalities that were present that day and enabled you to do the deal or provide exceptional service will probably be identifiable in your voice vibration. As you play back the tape, you may be able to distinguish your Business Person, your Closer, your Superb Customer Service Person or your Deal Maker. Listen to the words you used and what intonations you put on certain phrases. Breathe it in and take yourself back to that moment when you were fully on the Business Channel.

This is the first stage where you psych yourself and get in the appropriate state of mind. The second stage is to include the more rational part of your mind to ensure that you cover all the things that you have been trained to do. Now is the time to go over your checklist of these items to jog your memory. The checklist might include such things as the advantages and benefits of your product or services—and any special pricing consideration and so on.

Ready for Action

By now you should be feeling focused and clear. When you feel ready, make the call. The knowledge that you have done the necessary preparation and are totally one-minded about concluding the deal will boost the confidence you feel as you talk to your client.

This process of being one-minded and focusing on the channel appropriate to the situation is a very effective way of living your life. Relationships tend to improve as well because you give whomever you are with your full and undivided attention during the time you are together. Your partner, children, family and friends will probably appreciate having your undivided attention. Certainly your clients and colleagues will notice the difference too.

Channels of Consciousness

There is an abundance of channel frequencies on which you can operate your life. The ability to establish and maintain One-Mindedness is truly a key to balance and success.

Have you ever been on vacation at a beautiful location with someone you love and spent the whole time worrying about a particular deal or what's going on in the office? Two weeks can pass by and you don't even notice your surroundings, let alone the people you are with.

In Greece on a holiday, while we were driving around Athens, our taxi driver told us all about a wonderful waterfront restaurant owned by a dear friend of his family. His friend's mother was the cook and he said that at this restaurant we would be able to savor Greek home cooking at its best. He asked if we would allow him to make the arrangements for what would be a very special evening, one in which we would be treated just like family. It sounded like a real treat and we said we would be delighted to have him make the reservation for us.

That night we went to the restaurant. Just as our driver had said, it was in a magical spot on the water. We were greeted like long lost friends and shown to a waterfront table. We ordered our appetizers and sat back to watch the sun set over the bay. All in all, it promised to be a delightful evening.

While we were waiting for the food to arrive, another couple approached our table. They appeared agitated and we were somewhat taken aback when they told us they were leaving and that we should too. They said that the food was terrible and grossly overpriced. Their voices got louder and louder as they expressed their indignation at the fact that they had even been served wine out of already opened bottles.

Now, at this stage we had not experienced anything to suggest that their version of events was correct. However, we thanked them for the warning and they departed. Not content to simply take their word for it, we decided to wait for our first course. When it arrived, the food was passable but not as tasty as we had enjoyed on previous evenings at the local tavern. Then the wine waiter came and, just as the other tourists had warned, he began to pour us wine from already opened bottles.

At that point we decided to leave. I paid the bill, which came to three times what we'd paid the night before. I was so angry about this betrayal of trust by the taxi driver, that we walked the one mile or so back to the hotel, fuming and indignant. I continued obsessively raging about the whole experience of being ripped off all the next day and the next. On the third day my wife reminded me in her gentle way that I was no longer on holiday with her. She said my obsessing was an expensive hobby and she would like me back—enjoying beautiful Greece with her.

This is a real life example of how I had the skills and had forgotten to use them. It also illustrates the addictive nature of obsessive thinking. I had allowed negative, angry thoughts about this experience to consume precious holiday time. As I said before, we are 100% in control and can make a decision to change our obsessive thinking. It is helpful when we have a loving partner or peer support person who can keep reminding us of the choices we have available. Once again I was on the Vacation Channel.

One-Mindedness means the ability to be fully on the Vacation Channel when relaxing on vacation and fully on the Dollar-Productive Business Channel once you have returned to work. Like any new skill or habit, it takes a little time and practice to get really good at switching channels. But once you do, I'm sure you will notice how rewarding life can be.

Catalysts to One-Mindedness

The power of One-Mindedness is that it allows us to be at our optimum, 10/10 state—there are many catalysts to achieving this, including meditation, visualization, Inner Movie Theater and ritual.

State-Bound Consciousness

In a famous experiment, some medical students were each given eight ounces of vodka and then trained in a particular laboratory procedure involving the making of sample tissue slides. It was not a simple task but neither was it especially daunting.

The next day, when they were stone cold sober, the same students were unable to perform the procedure. It was like the training had been a dream and now that dream had evaporated. They were then given vodka again and they performed the task perfectly. The alcohol took them back to the tissue slide-making channel that they couldn't access when sober.

We call this condition State-Bound Consciousness. When I am in the United States, I find great difficulty remembering details of street names and places in Christchurch, New Zealand. As soon as I get back to New Zealand, that information is almost magically available in my mind once more.

So it's not unusual to find that things learned in a particular state or channel of consciousness can be recalled best with the emotion and ambience of the time when they were originally learned. For example, I learned Italian when I was studying Hebrew at the University of Jerusalem. At the time this meant that I could only access my Italian vocabulary when on my Hebrew Channel.

Retirement and Alzheimer's

When I work with people who are retired, I notice they have often moved to a state of consciousness where they have forgotten how to strive. Former high-achieving top executives suddenly find themselves with no new challenges. In effect, their channel selection has diminished—almost overnight—from being a smorgasbord of choices to being merely one or two. Their days become predictable: getting up, making breakfast, reading the newspaper, playing golf, eating dinner, going to bed. If retirement becomes limiting in this way, I have seen formerly vibrant, interesting people aging dramatically and suddenly becoming little old people.

The message is clear—don't ever stop striving. In my own life, I do something every year that I might have once considered impossible. Whether it is a trip to India that takes me completely out of my comfort zone or learning a new sport or skill, I consider taking on new challenges to be not only part of the adventure of life but also the Fountain of Youth.

Alzheimer's disease, on the other hand, is about losing the ability to access the channels of consciousness you need. This is analogous to losing whole drawers of your filing system, or the hard drive on your computer crashing and all the data being lost. A person suffering from Alzheimer's might greet her nurse like a long-lost friend but fail to recognize her own spouse or child.

Activities like playing bridge, writing your life story, doing crossword puzzles—whatever it takes to keep your mind active and sharp—are like regularly servicing a clock to keep it ticking along nicely.

Transitions

Sometimes an individual can have difficulty in moving smoothly and painlessly from one channel of consciousness to another. People who exhibit these tendencies can have difficulty relaxing and are often jumpy, restless or easily distracted. If this is allowed to escalate into extreme perfectionism or nervousness it can interfere with performance. For instance, the child who consistently shoots baskets at home may be unable to shoot goals in a real game because his nervousness has turned into stress. If the basketball player is unable to channel this surge of energy, using it as speed and stamina for the game, it can radically impede his performance.

I had a European client once who was taking oral exams before a select committee of his professors in order to qualify to practice medicine in Belgium. An extreme perfectionist, this man employed me to teach him how to relax so he could perform at optimum levels on the test and not blank out from test anxiety. Using the Inner Movie Theater I taught him how to breathe deeply and to be relaxed while on the Exam Channel. He was able to pass his test and achieve his goal of becoming a doctor.

In my own life I experience this each time I prepare to do a presentation. To do this I need to go onto my Speaker Channel. I have learned to arrive at a speaking venue several hours before the engagement so I have time to get onto the channel without being interrupted and thrown off track.

Know Yourself

The real value of understanding One-Mindedness, sub-personalities and your own personal channel selector is that it opens a whole universe of possibilities for your life. By understanding how you operate, you can design a framework of personal channels for your own inner television set, as well as a whole catalogue of tapes to run in your Inner Movie Theater to assist your transition between channels and to minimize stress.

In other words, you are using more of your mind's capabilities to tap into and create the Magnificent Life you have always wanted. Effectively, you are well on the way to Black Belt status.

EXERCISE ONE

The Awareness Continuum

Using a stopwatch and timing yourself for one minute, bring your focus of awareness to the foreground. Say out loud, "Now I am aware that…" and describe what you are aware of. Every few seconds, move to what is now in the foreground of your Awareness Continuum. When the minute is up, give yourself a one-minute break and then repeat the exercise. Do it three times. In the space below make any comments or impressions you have about this experience.

EXERCISE TWO

Designing a Tape for My Inner Movie Theater

Choose any channel from your personal selection and create an audiotape for it. Before you record your tape, you might like to jog your memory by brainstorming a particular experience. Go back to the happiest moment you have ever known on the channel you have selected. If it is Channel 22, the Family Channel, you might recall the first time you told your beloved how much you loved him or her. Or it might be the time he or she told you how much you are loved. How did it feel? Remember to evoke all your senses (visual, olfactory, auditory and tactile) and emotions. Jot down words and phrases as they occur to you, without judging them in any way.

When you are fully back in that moment, feeling again how wonderful it was, switch on your tape recorder and speak into it. Later, as you play it back to yourself, see if you can identify any of the sub-personalities that are speaking through you. This process of sub-personality identification is a skill that can be developed by everyone.

Make as many tapes for as many different channels as you choose. Use these tapes in your morning ritual and to aid transitions from channel to channel as you go through your daily activities.

Channel:

Tape Entitled:

6

Mastering the Channels

*"Where love rules there is no will to power and
where power predominates, love is lacking.
The one is a shadow of the other." Carl Jung*

Owning Your Television Channels

Have you ever wanted to be a media mogul and own your own television channels? In this chapter you will have the opportunity to do exactly that.

In Chapter Five we discussed the potential channels we have in our minds and how they might be harnessed in such a way that we live life more successfully—whatever the word "successful" means within the context of our own lives. In this chapter are some skills and techniques that I have been using with my clients to assist them in developing the channels of their minds. In the exercises at the end of this chapter, you will be given the opportunity to play with the concept of having your own personal channel selector and deciding what will go on it. Have fun!

Your Private Channel Selector

Imagine you have a remote control for all the channels you want to use in your mind. What channels might be on your personal channel selector? Perhaps you could have a channel for family, one for being a lover, another for work, a separate one for golf, another for driving, yet another for going to a concert and so on. The list is endless.

Fred's Bread-Making Channel

I love the whole process of baking bread, so I have a special Bread-Making Channel that I've labeled Channel 23. The Bread-Making Channel is one I switch to on a regular basis when I'm home. Preparing and mixing the ingredients, baking the loaves in the oven, smelling that delicious aroma wafting through my home, watching the loaves rise, taking them out of the oven and letting them cool down enough to sample—the whole procedure is one that engages all of my senses and many of my sub-personalities.

My Organizer makes sure I have the finest ingredients for my specialty loaves. My Child just loves the naughtiness of picking out the sultanas and tasting the other ingredients, such as ginger. My Chemist enjoys figuring out new combinations of flavors and grains to use. My Nurturer loves to give away the loaves to people and see the pleasure they get from such an unexpected and individualized gift.

I even have my own label for the bread that says, "Bread by Fred, Made Especially for You." I love to see the thrill people get out of receiving a loaf of bread that I have designed especially with them in mind. As you can probably tell from my enthusiasm, when I am on the Bread-Making Channel, I am totally one-minded about the activity of baking bread.

A Note about Sub-Personalities

As we discussed in Chapter One, the Swiss psychologist Carl Jung first coined the term sub-personalities. In working with your own sub-personalities, it is important to realize that any sub-personality can turn up on any channel at any time. It is very important to ensure we bring the appropriate sub-personalities to a particular task on a particular channel. For instance, the Child is usually not Dollar-Productive, so is not appropriate on Channel 37 when we are in business mode. When you are feeling that you are 10/10 in any given situation, you can feel confident that the most appropriate sub-personalities are on that channel.

While you are reading through the channel selector later in this chapter, you might like to think about which sub-personalities are appropriate to each channel. To help you, here is a list of sub-personalities and some common phrases they might use. In reading through this list, you might want to make a note of any that seem very familiar to you, any that you should pay attention to as a signal to change channels and any new ones that you would like to add to the list.

Salesperson: "I wouldn't do this deal for anyone else, but I'll do it for you." "This design is very popular, so you'd better hurry." "I don't need your money." "I'm doing this just for you."

Manager: "Here's what we need to do." "Well, the first item on the agenda is ..."

Yuppie: "Have you seen his car? It's a really snazzy BMW Z4 with racing alloys and a satellite navigation system." "Look at my new wristwatch with all the latest gadgets." "You should see the new phone I'm going to buy."

Minister: "This is part of God's curriculum for you. How can I help?"

Planner: "For this to happen, we're going to need to do X, Y, Z ..." "If I get this done by 5pm today then I can ..." "Our plan for this year is ..."

Businessperson: "What kind of return will I get for my investment of time/money/energy?"

Organizer: "First things first. OK, how about if you do ..."

Fine Human Being: "You are an amazing human being." "How can I help you?"

Wise Person: "From the historical perspective ..." "I know of a situation ..." "There are several ways we can look at this ..." "Do you want a piece of unsolicited advice?"

Aware Witness: "That's interesting ..." "While you were speaking, I sensed a great happiness coming from you."

Take Charge/Can Do Person: "Just leave it to me."

Rule Setter: "Now if you want to get ahead in this job you're going to need to ..." "Here is the correct way we should do it ..."

Person of Integrity: "You've given me too much change. It should be $2, not $10." "Thank you."

Assertive Person/Achiever: "You've come to the right person. When do we start?"

Creative Person: "Let's try looking at this from a different perspective ..."

Adventurer: "Why not?" "Yes, yes, yes!"

Pusher: "You'd better ... or else!" "More, do more!" "You won't get it done in time." "It's not enough, we need more."

Judge: "How dare you!" "That kind of attitude is not acceptable here!" "You should be ashamed of yourself."

Worrier: "What if they don't like my presentation? I just know I'll blow it!"

Doubter: "I don't think this will work." "No, I'm sure it will fall apart."

Gossip: "Did you know that X was cheating on his wife?"

Procrastinator: "I've got too much on my plate right now; I'll get to it later."

Comedian: "Did you hear the one about ..."

Avoider: "Don't tell me, I don't want to know about it."

Guilty Person: "I shouldn't have done that; I've let them all down." "I knew I wouldn't get it right. I never do."

Cynic: "Yeah, I've heard that one before!" "Tell me something new." "Tell me something I don't know."

Scarer: "Be careful ... if you don't ... might happen." "Watch out!" "Looks like cancer to me. Have you got life insurance?"

Poor Girl/Boy: "That's very expensive. Why don't we wait until it's on sale?" "I don't really need it. I can sew up the tear."

Catastrophizer: "It'll never work. Something always goes wrong." "We can't park here; we'll get in trouble with the police."

Humiliator: "Who do you think you are?" "You're a liar." "How dare you!" "You idiot, you jerk!"

Blamer/Not Me: "Wasn't me. I'd never do such a thing. Must have been Joe."

Skeptic: "There's got to be a catch somewhere; it's just too good to be true. Read the small print."

Perfectionist: "Nobody else will do it as well as me." "I failed. I only got 98% on my test." "I still have more to do; I'll never get it done in time."

Your Channels

The following list describes channels common to many of us. You might want to browse through it and decide which of the channels are appropriate for you. You may also start to identify channels that are personal to you and the things you enjoy. You may notice that these often reflect the 10s, 25s and so on that have been discussed earlier.

Later you will have the opportunity to identify and design your own personal channels; both those that you can start using immediately and those that you can have in readiness for new experiences and adventures. You might add those personal channels to the list below. Please note that the following list of channels of consciousness is by no means exhaustive and that is why you need to identify or design your own. Also, the numbers and names allocated to the channels are to be used as guides—feel free to number or label yours as you choose.

A Quick Guide to the Channels of Consciousness

Here are some of the channels that I have identified. The ideal is to place each type of experience on different and appropriate channels. When we can do that, we then move easily from activity to activity in a relaxed state of One-Mindedness.

The first one hundred channels are what I call ordinary reality. Once you get beyond Channel 100, you move into the realms of telepathy, healing and telekinesis. For now we will focus on the ordinary reality channels, 1 to 100. Everyone can learn and do this.

Channels 1, 2 and 3: Entertainment and News Channels

These are the Small Poppy and Child Channels. Most of us have been trained to believe that these are the only channels that exist and attempt to do everything on them. As a result, we often feel stressed and overwhelmed. Think of stress as being like the static on your TV set when you cannot get the exact frequency for a particular station. Like a fuzzy TV picture, stress makes it difficult for us to focus and makes us susceptible to distractions and interruptions.

Channel 9: Play Channel (Peter Pan Channel)

This is the channel we turn to when we want to engage in some child-like fun. Water fights, tickling, pillow fights; these are all examples of fun in which we, as adults, can safely engage with our Child sub-personality. Inappropriate sub-personalities on this channel include the Judge, the Accountant and the Lover.

Channel 20: Love/Romance Channel

This is the channel for romance, when love and sex are in the air. On this channel we engage in mating behavior, including flirting and seduction.

Channel 22: Family Channel

This is the channel for home, family and beloveds. On this channel we express our love and respect for the special people in our lives. In return we feel loved, secure and contented.

Not too long ago, I heard a beautiful story about a family—mom, dad and two children—who were out to dinner together. At the end of the meal, the father went to each family member, starting with his daughter who was about three years old. He lifted her out of her seat and into his arms. As she snuggled into his chest, he kissed her cheek and told her how special she was. He thanked her for being his daughter. He then handed her to his wife, who sat the little girl on her lap. The father sat in the seat vacated by his daughter and turned his full attention to his son, who was about eight years old. He put his arm around the boy's shoulder and gazed deeply into his eyes. He smiled and then, in a quiet voice, he told his son how proud he was of him and how wonderful it was to have him as his son. The boy beamed with delight at this praise.

Finally, the man took his daughter from his wife's knee and placed her back on her seat. He held out his hand to his wife and she stood up. He touched her cheek and told her he loved her. Then he embraced her in a warm and loving kiss.

As the family prepared to pay the bill and go home, the maitre d' was heard to ask if it was some special family occasion. The man replied that yes, it was very special because it was a night with the people who meant the most to him. He added that it wasn't a birthday or anniversary. The maitre d' then asked how long the couple had been together. The wife responded that they had been married for 12 years. The maitre d' looked astonished as he replied that he himself was newly married. He went on to say that he hoped he would still feel as lovingly about his partner in 12 years. The man responded, "Don't hope, sir, decide."

Channel 23: Relaxation Channel

This is the hobby channel. This is the channel I am on when making bread. Learning another language, learning to dance, taking singing or bridge lessons—all of these activities are on Channel 23.

Channel 24: Sports Channel

This is the channel for active sport and outdoor activities like hiking, bike riding, basketball, tennis, golf, football, baseball and soccer. It is the channel where we are actively engaged rather than just spectators watching others play.

Channel 33: Wisdom Channel

This is where we develop and meet with our Inner Mastermind and Outer Mastermind group. It is where we develop the perspective of the Elder, Knower, Wise Person and Sage.

Channel 37: Dollar-Productive Business Channel

This is the channel we use for business. When we are on this channel, we engage in Dollar-Productive activities; that is, the activities that we have identified as being the ones that earn us the highest income. We will be looking at this channel in more detail in Chapter Eight.

Channel 38: Assistant Channel

Everyone needs an assistant, yet sometimes we do the work of an assistant ourselves. This is the channel that is often confused with the Dollar-Productive Business Channel. On Channel 38 we do busy work when we are meant to be on Channel 37. This includes such tasks as filing, cleaning, organizing staff, and so on. On Channel 38 our hourly wage drops dramatically to 10% to 15% of Channel 37 income. By employing an assistant to take care of these tasks, we could have more time to devote to Channel 37 and Dollar-Productive activities. On the Assistant Channel, we are 5 out of 10.

Channel 49: Celebration Channel

This is where we get our heart's desires and celebrate the Magnificent Life. When we are on this channel, we are engaged in the activities that bring us great joy (the 10s, 25s, 50s and 100s), that fill our hearts and souls with great happiness. Holidays, festivals and major life events such as getting married and having a long-awaited baby happen on this channel.

Channel 50: Knowledge Channel

This is where we store new learning. At times it can get buried in our unconscious until some reminder system brings it to the surface. This new knowledge then needs to be switched to an active channel. This is like information stored on the hard drive of a computer. It is in using this stored material that we really discover its worth.

Channel 69: Dysfunctional Channel

Behavior on this channel is not apparently constructive or beneficial to a loving, healthy, happy life. It is the one we go to when we are feeling depressed or oppressed (victim). On this channel we feel unworthy and have feelings of low self-esteem, guilt, fear and worry. Our minds are crowded with thoughts about what we shouldn't have done or said. On this channel we create judgment, blame, and despair. The only thing we create on this channel is negativity.

Channel 69 B: Hallucination Channel

A subsection of the Dysfunctional Channel, Channel 69 B is what I call the Hallucination or the Coma Channel. This is where we go to avoid dealing with our current reality. When we are on this channel, we tend to drink alcohol, watch TV, take drugs, mope, gamble and procrastinate. It is a way of not noticing how we are living our lives.

Channel 73: Party Channel

Channel 73 is where we go to let off steam. Known as the Party Channel or Bacchanalia (named after Bacchus, the Greek God of wine and revelry), this channel allows us to blow off excess energy in a group setting. It is also a Participation Channel where the individual becomes actively involved. It is not the same to watch the scenes of revelry at Times Square on New Year's Eve on television, as it is to be there. To enjoy the magic, it is important to be part of that group energy. Life is not a spectator sport, participation is essential.

The thing to remember about the Party Channel is that a little goes a long way. In other words, if we visit it a couple of times a year on designated occasions such as New Year's Eve, Mardi Gras and the Harvest Festival, then it serves a useful purpose. However, if we visit the Party Channel every weekend, then it may start to wreak havoc with our health, ability to perform at work and our relationships.

It is inappropriate to take your sub-personalities of Accountant or Worrier along with you to Mardi Gras, because they will definitely get in the way of you having a good time.

Channel 77: Dream Channel

The Dream Channel is the one on which we connect with alternative realities that we would like to create in our lives. The way we do this is through dreams, visions and the use of active imagination through visualization. The Inner Movie Theater technique is an example of this.

Channel 99: New Habit Channel

Channel 99 is the one that designs and implements habit creation. From this channel we format new channels. Channel 99 is the one we use to take a vision from the dream state on Channel 77 and design the habit patterns to make that vision a concrete goal. Next we want to establish and create an Eight Point Plan to make the new habit a reality.

Making the Transition Between Channels

As we have discovered, the key to One-Mindedness is learning how to switch fully OFF one channel and ON to a new channel. When we switch to a new channel, we are, at the same time, changing our mood, our perspective and our attitude. Once we have mastered this we can successfully move from activity to activity and achieve close to, if not total, 10/10 presence. Let's use the techniques we have already identified to see how this might be achieved.

Let's imagine you are a single, female real estate agent. All day you have been on Channel 37, the Business Channel. You have been totally absorbed in business for eight hours, making client calls and prospecting. It is now 5pm and it is time to start getting ready for a big date that you have that evening. It is time to make the transition to Channel 20, the Love Channel, because the last thing you want to do is go on your date still thinking about work. Your new love interest will probably lose his enthusiasm for you very quickly if all you can talk about is business. He will also be able to sense if you are not fully present because your mind is elsewhere—wondering how you are going to approach the owner of the one million dollar property that you would love to list for auction.

The first thing to assist you in making the transition to the Love Channel might be to replay the tapes you have of how you met this man, conversations you have had with him and previous dates you have enjoyed together. Now you are ready to move more and more into being 10/10 present for your date.

Advertising companies are experts at moving us from channel to channel. Think about the instant recognition children have for the golden arches of the MacDonald's logo or the reaction your salivary glands have when you are in a shopping center and you smell the aroma of freshly baked cookies. The advertisers hope that your instant physiological response will lead you to buy their product. This conscious manipulation is the same Top of Mind Awareness technique we can use in a mindful and conscious way to serve our best interests, to take us from one channel to another at will.

In summary, breathing deeply, meditating, creative visualization, Inner Movie Theater and ritual are all techniques and skills for moving off one channel and onto another. Once you are on a new channel, it should have your Top of Mind Awareness. You can test whether or not you have achieved this by asking yourself, "On a scale of 1 to 10, how present am I right now." If you score yourself 5 or under, use any of the techniques to bring yourself into a more relaxed state and, when this is done, rate yourself once more. Keep going until you score 8 or above.

Have fun playing with One-Mindedness on your different channels and start to notice how it can enhance your life. The exercises at the end of the chapter are designed to assist you in getting comfortable with the techniques introduced in this chapter.

Unconscious Stress

As discussed, on Channels 1, 2 and 3 we might feel stressed and overwhelmed. Many times we have an unconscious stress reaction that is an involuntary response out of proportion to the situation we are in at the time. If you and I are sitting and chatting over a cup of coffee and you are experiencing stress, then your body is creating a physiological response to some memory that has been triggered or there is fear about some future event. Again, by choosing to access your Inner Movie Theater, you can move yourself out of this uncomfortable situation. The art of the Inner Movie Theater is to have prepared a selection of videos to use to transform any potentially stressful situation into a neutral state. Remember, you can control your Inner Movie Theater, you can regulate your oxygen intake and you can measure stress.

Stress-o-meter Measurements

The Stress-o-meter is what I have used to help my clients deal with stress.

Yellow Range: 0 to 15. Very relaxed, laid back and even sleepy. In this range you feel little or no stress at all. For example, when you fall asleep, your stress level might measure 0. This range is appropriate for meditation and sleep but not for achieving tasks.

Green Range: 15 to 30. This is the normal range that people operate in most of the time. When in this range, you feel that life is good and full of opportunity, and tasks are performed easily.

Blue Range: 30 to 50. In this range you might still feel generally on top of things, yet the moments of worry and feelings of being under pressure are becoming more frequent.

Red Range: 50 to 70. In this range you are no longer feeling on top of things. You are feeling stressed and your body is experiencing symptoms such as headaches, neck ache, backache, stomach upsets and so on.

Flashing Red Range: 70 to 100. At the high end of the scale, this is the sort of stress associated with being rushed to hospital in an ambulance with a medical emergency. This is the danger zone where such physiological conditions as heart attacks and strokes occur.

The Ideal Range is between 20 and 30 on the Stress-o-meter. This range is where you operate normally. Once you calculate your stress level at 45 or above, your body is likely to start experiencing physiological symptoms.

How to Use the Stress-o-meter

Take a deep breath and then ask yourself, "On a scale of 1 to 100, how stressed am I feeling, right now?" You might have just enjoyed a good night's sleep; you're feeling refreshed and ready for the day. You might put your stress measurement between 15 and 30.

At regular intervals throughout the day and evening, continue to check in and monitor your stress level. Perhaps you arrive at the office and find the alarm is going off. What is your stress level now? The security people arrive and it is ascertained that nothing has been disturbed and probably the alarm is faulty. What is your stress level now? Keep breathing and checking yourself throughout the day.

Using the Inner Movie Theater

By the use of a technique we discussed in Chapter Five, called the Inner Movie Theater, we can also consciously adjust stress. The Inner Movie Theater involves the use of active imagination. By the process of imagining, we can move our mind to a variety of experiences. Let's try it right now.

Take a deep breath, and then imagine yourself being present in a hug from your daughter or a kiss from your lover, or anything else from your list of 10s. Now give yourself a measurement on the Stress-o-meter. Are you in the green range? Yellow? On the scale of 1 to 100, what would your measurement be? Hopefully your body has moved to a delightful, calm response that you can measure. Your heart rate might have actually slowed and if we were to measure your blood pressure, it might have decreased.

Pink Fairy Bike

Here's an example from when I worked with a realtor who owns his own business. His company has enjoyed a remarkable year with extremely good results. He is a very serious man, very sober, almost a philosopher or college professor type. As he spoke about his company, he talked very knowledgeably about gross and net profits, just like any good accountant might.

Then we talked about the Christmas presents he had bought for his children, aged three and one. His voice got very animated as he told me how his little girl had been asking Santa for a pink bike with fairies. As he described searching the whole city for a pink bike with fairies on it, he stopped being the accountant and even the businessman and was fully in his sub-personality of loving dad.

The elation in his voice when he told me he finally found the highly-prized pink bike with fairies was an absolute delight to hear. For the rest of the session, whenever he got too serious I said, "Tell me a little more about the pink bike with fairies on it," and immediately he switched to being the delighted daddy who had come home with the dream bike for his little girl.

Just as this client could change his mood and stress level each time he heard *pink bike with fairies* you can learn to switch your mood. Stress is a dysfunctional response to a life challenge and an internal response to a life situation. An unhealthy response to stress creates physiological symptoms in the body, such as elevated heart rate and blood pressure. The body has these physiological responses to ready itself for fight or flight. Chronic or prolonged stress can be potentially dangerous to the sufferer, because it might result in a stroke or a variety of other health problems.

Many people believe they are feeling stressed because something external to themselves has caused them to feel this way. Actually, it's an internal process, and they have a lot more control of their own responses than they realize. The Stress-o-meter is a tool that enables people to develop greater control when they are feeling discomfort and stress.

Exercise One

Part A

From the following list of activities, choose four or five that you would find pleasurable. For each of the five, design a channel appropriate for it, using the bullet point list in Part B.

1. Walking along the sand of a tropical beach on a balmy summer's night.
2. Making love to your beloved (in the present or the future) in a beautiful, candlelit room with soft music playing in the background.
3. Watching your first child being born.
4. Getting a hole-in-one during a round of golf.
5. Negotiating the biggest deal of your career.
6. Employing a really efficient, pleasant assistant to take care of your administrative tasks.
7. Taking your family to Europe for a long-anticipated six-week holiday.
8. Receiving your degree on graduation day from the Dean of a University.
9. Exchanging vows with your beloved as you become life partners.
10. Setting up your own business after you have dreamed of taking such a step for many years.

Part B

For each scene above that you visualized, use the bullet point list below to design a channel on which you can place it.

- Number of channel
- Name of channel
- Purpose of channel
- Sub-personalities on this channel
- Sub-personalities to avoid on this channel
- Best time to use this channel
- How I might switch to this channel

Exercise Two

The "Stress-o-meter"

The aim of this exercise is to practice moving your mind at will. Scene One is designed to help you find a peaceful place within yourself that you can return to at any time.

Scene One

Imagine a peaceful, relaxing scene in which you feel nurtured and safe. Breathe deeply and then measure your stress level on a scale of 1 to 100. Ideally, it will be in the 20 to 30 range or below. This is now your baseline, the place you can return to at any time. When you are ready—move to Scene Two.

Scene Two

You are driving home from work. As you get near your street, you notice several fire trucks and police cars passing you with their sirens blaring and red lights flashing. You turn into your street and you realize it is your house that is burning. You pull to the curb, jump out of your car and stand helplessly, watching your house burn to the ground. What is your stress level now? Breathe deeply and comfortably.

Scene Three

Now you realize you can't see any of your beloveds. Your partner, your children, your pets—where are they? What is your stress level now? Breathe deeply and comfortably.

Return to your Scene One. Breathe deeply and comfortably. Measure your stress level. Continue breathing and measuring until your stress level returns to your normal range.

7

Beliefs about Wealth

"Nobody, as long as he moves about among the chaotic currents of life, is without trouble." Carl Jung.

What Is a Belief?

The Oxford Dictionary defines a belief as acceptance of something as true. Beliefs are personal to each one of us. Many of my beliefs will be different from what you believe, even though there may be some similarities and areas of overlap. Not only are beliefs personal, they are also dynamic, not static, and many have a "use-by-date." We can decide at any time that a belief no longer serves us, and change it.

A belief is a mind habit as opposed to a body habit, but that does not mean that it is hard wired into our bio-computer. For example, a 19-year-old soldier in World War I might have been a pacifist before he found himself in the trenches facing a hostile enemy. That belief would no longer serve him if it was his desire to stay alive. Faced with killing or being killed, he might decide that his new belief was, "I will protect myself and stay alive, whatever it takes."

Hypostasis and Truth

A belief, therefore, is something that you accept. An hypostasis is something that you not only accept; you are also prepared to make an investment in it. For example, my belief is that I will live until I am 120 years old. I won't know whether my belief is true until I reach the age of 121. An hypostasis takes a belief—"I will live until I am 120 years old"—and

113

elevates it to truth <u>for me</u>. An hypostasis also presents me with a challenge by asking what I am going to do to assist this new belief in becoming a reality. Whatever action I decide to take, such as ensuring I care for my physical body with good nutrition and appropriate exercise and setting up a financial plan to ensure I will be able to live in the standard I require until the day I die—all of these actions reflect my level of commitment.

Truth, according to my belief, is something that is eternal and in the realm of God. That is, God knows truth and so does our angelic nature. During our incarnations here on earth, we deal with contextual truths. For instance, "Killing is wrong, except in self-defense." Beliefs are constructs of this finite realm, truth is of the infinite.

Shifting Core Beliefs

Have you noticed that the work we have been doing so far is really about becoming very conscious about how you live each moment of this precious life you have been given? There is a popular song from the recent movie *Great Expectations* that has the lyrics: "The future is a mistress that is so hard to please; the past is a pebble in my shoe. Today's the day."

These words remind us of the importance of being fully present right now and ideally all the time, on the channel appropriate for the moment. To have a 10/10 experience throughout our day, we have to decide what channel of consciousness we want to be on at any given time and maintain our focus of awareness until we allow ourselves or decide to switch to another channel. Sometimes when going along on a particular day of life, my Soul Partner takes over and I catch myself doing something other than what I had intended to do. Often I decide that the new activity is actually better than what I was previously doing so I go with it. This is an example of my ever-watchful Soul Partner taking over and expressing himself.

Becoming this conscious allows us to be very clear about how we want our life to look. It also empowers us to design a Magnificent Life worthy of an Incarnate Angel. As you work more and more with this expanded view of who you are, you may find yourself being more challenged by core beliefs that no longer serve you and need to be upgraded.

You may be starting to find that certain beliefs no longer sit well with you. Imagine it like this: you have gone shopping in the Belief store to find some new beliefs. Down one aisle you find the Peripheral Belief section, and it is here that you pick out some beliefs about yourself that have more entertainment value than real significance. For example, you might decide to select the belief that the color blue suits you. Down the next aisle you notice that the prices on each of the beliefs are significantly higher than in the peripheral section.

If you want to own a new belief, you have to really invest in it. You find a belief that looks really attractive, such as I'm going to live until I'm 120 years old. The price that you have to pay for it includes setting up your finances to last well past the average lifespan. Then you must maintain your optimum physical and mental prowess with exercise, good nutrition and keeping your mind active. Once you truly invest energy, thought, new habits, time and money into a new belief, it is on its way to becoming a core belief for your life.

Changing core beliefs is an organic process. Just as your body is continuously creating new tissue, it is possible and desirable to continuously review and possibly revise your core beliefs.

The world is changing so quickly that those people who are unable to shift their core beliefs when circumstances demand it, can become stressed and feel out of touch.

Beliefs Have a Use-by-Date

Beliefs, like all other aspects of life, have a lifespan. They are instilled in us, they stay with us, and then they will either be renewed or become obsolete as their use-by-date passes. Just like cream or yogurt that has passed its use-by-date, beliefs that are obsolete will start to smell (metaphorically). Some people regard their beliefs as God-given and therefore eternal. They act as if their beliefs are hardwired and nothing can change them. For instance, I know a retired accountant who believes that he has no reason to learn the computer because a pen and paper work just fine.

While his wife has embraced new technology, he holds onto his old beliefs and in doing so, deprives himself of potential new activities in retirement.

If we regard changing our beliefs as a natural process and choose to make an adventure out of it, rather than hanging onto the good old days, then it can be an exciting and dynamic process. For instance, for the first 15 years of my life I held onto the belief that fatter people were healthier and that a skinny person obviously could not afford food; that his or her family were not good providers. In my own immigrant tradition, food played an extremely important role and refusal to eat everything on your plate was regarded as a grievous sin. In my teens I realized girls were not attracted to fat boys and lean and mean was far sexier. Because I was interested in girls, I soon shifted my core belief.

Voluntary or Involuntary

One of the certainties of life is that it will change. What you experience today is not necessarily how it will be tomorrow. We have a choice to adapt to changing circumstances and create a life on purpose or struggle when change is imposed on us. War, famine, flood, earthquakes, the death of a loved one, receiving a diagnosis of cancer—these are all examples of change being imposed on us through new circumstances over which we have little or no control. In fact, one of the major causes of stress is an inability to cope with rapid change.

Different Speeds

What happens if people are in stable relationships, yet they are growing at different speeds and there is the potential for one to leave the other behind? I have noticed some patterns to the way partners might choose to deal with this.

One possible course of action is for the one who is changing to make the decision not to grow any further. Another possibility, especially in a marriage or a love relationship, is to know when you and your beloved are going through an accelerated moment to fulfill your destiny—and to accept that you may grow at different rates. The experience of growing does not have to be in the same area. For instance, if your spouse's parent dies, your beloved may go through an extended period of grief and that may put pressure on your relationship. The acceptance that this is part of your partner's journey may help you extend the support needed at this time. This may also mean giving them space to deal with their loss in their own way.

When people attend personal development courses, I encourage them to invite their partners and spouses. Even if they choose not to take an active part themselves, it is important that they have some level of understanding of the potentially transformational process their beloved is undergoing. This can help maintain communication between a couple even if they are progressing on their life path at different rates.

Negotiating Differences

Some things, such as time spent on different activities, can be negotiated. Being able to negotiate time spent in activities that aren't necessarily our first choice yet please our partner can be a quid pro quo. This means trading something of value for something else of value that enables each partner to feel they are being honored in the relationship.

This is different from a bribe. When a husband is having an affair and his wife finds out, he may buy her a diamond ring to keep her pacified and maintain the stability of the relationship—a bribe doesn't solve the problem, it distracts from it. The bully husband, who in the same situation tells her to get over it does not solve the situation either, but pushes it underground. This is avoidance, not quid pro quo.

Here is an example of quid pro quo featuring two people with honorable intentions. When working with a couple from Arizona, I found that they were experiencing challenges around his desire to go skiing every weekend. While the husband loved going to the ski slopes and was a highly proficient skier, his wife hated the mountains. She would stay at home and feel lonely and resentful. He missed her company yet didn't want to give up his sporting passion.

This couple loved each other and truly wanted to find a resolution. When I asked the wife what she would like in return for accompanying her husband on every second or third ski trip, she responded that she wanted a new car. A new car seemed to honor her value in the relationship and, of course, offered her freedom and mobility. The car, however, wasn't a lasting solution because it was a bribe. Soon she was once again experiencing loneliness and isolation on the weekends when her husband was skiing. Eventually she negotiated a membership in an exclusive country club and he committed to going with her every Thursday evening—making this a real quid pro quo. Throughout this challenge both people remained firmly committed to each other and their relationship.

A third possibility is equal and opposite. This is really when the partners have desires and dreams that are opposing. An example of this might be when one partner wants to have a baby but the other does not. This is an either/or situation—in other words, you can't have a baby and not have a baby. The challenge for a couple making this choice is much more difficult because it requires shifting core beliefs.

Changing Old Core Beliefs to New Core Beliefs

Your thoughts and the words you speak are clues to what it is you really believe and hold dear. Let's examine the real life example of Sue and Joe. We worked together to shift core beliefs that were no longer supporting their relationship. These included beliefs about themselves, marriage, parenthood and wealth.

At the time we met, Sue was 43 years old and married to Joe, a former car salesman. They had two children, aged 10 and 12. Sue grew up in a poor family and had adopted the core beliefs of poor boy/poor girl. She was very close to her family and the cultural beliefs held by her family included that the children come first and that a good wife has a spotless home and knows how to make a little go a long way.

Joe started his career in car sales working for others, on a low base salary and commission. During this period Sue excelled as a homemaker, making do on very little money and using her skills to produce nutritious meals from cheap cuts of meat. An accomplished dressmaker, she also made clothes for herself and the children.

Sue liked to tell her friends and family, "I have to get a bargain or else I'm being ripped off," and "I only shop at sales time." She believed there was intrinsic value in getting a bargain. She would delay buying new items, even if they were needed, until they were offered at a reduced price. She cleaned the house herself to save money and not be out of line with the rules of her inner parent.

Ten years ago Joe opened his own business. An accomplished salesperson and astute businessman, he continued to expand, making the business a multimillion dollar enterprise. And yet, in Sue's mind, it was as if her husband was still earning $50,000 a year.

As the managing director, Joe had less of a hands-on approach to the business. Strategic planning, managing his staff and entertaining corporate clients were now essential elements of his role. He took up golf as a way of networking and cementing client relationships.

Sue, on the other hand, spent her days driving the children to their various activities. While they were at school, she cleaned the house, shopped and visited elderly members of the family. Joe told me in an early coaching session that he wanted his beloved wife to enjoy and benefit from the bounty that his business had been able to provide for them, including the many dinners they were invited to by clients. He had become increasingly embarrassed by her appearance and her obvious discomfort with eating in expensive restaurants. He would have loved to see the children wearing trendy clothes and going to the private schools.

Then the family moved to a large, new home in a more affluent suburb and Joe encouraged Sue to employ a cleaning person one day a week. Sue felt offended by the suggestion, because maintaining a spotless home had always been a source of great pride. Sue felt lonely in her new surroundings. She missed her old neighbors and the local shopkeepers.

The last straw came when Joe came home one night and told her they had been invited by his major client to go to Europe and to Scotland on a golfing tour. He suggested that she treat herself to some new outfits and take some golfing lessons. Sue did not want any part of this foolishness and wastefulness. She believed she needed to stay home and take care of the house and family. Sue felt that this trip would put her marriage under unbearable pressure. Both partners were feeling resentful at this stage and their sexual relationship had ceased.

New Beliefs and New Behavior

Joe and I were already working together in a coaching relationship. When Joe told me about Sue's reaction to the golfing trip, I suggested he ask Sue if she would like to have some combined sessions. After some initial hesitation she agreed.

At the first session I asked them how they felt about each other. Sue said that she really loved Joe and wanted to keep her marriage. Joe said that he loved her but that he was distressed about the lack of sex over the previous weeks and Sue's negative reaction to the European trip.

Daily Accountability

Although Sue and Joe loved each other, they didn't really talk. One of the first things I suggested they do was to share 10s with each other. Then they had to give each other half a day of 10s. This involved planning special treats for each other. For instance, Joe arranged for Sue to have a morning at a spa and Sue arranged for Joe to have a massage after his golf game. I also asked them to consider having a date night once a week and to arrange a babysitter.

Joe and Sue also agreed to keep a **Daily Accountability Chart**. This involved identifying the major areas in their lives, such as their relationship, time with the children, fitness and work. They were to set aside quiet time, preferably at the end of each day, to assess how they felt they were doing in these different aspects of their lives and for each category they were to allocate a score of 1 to 10. At the end of each week and then at the end of each month, they were to tally up their individual scores and average them.

This is Sue's chart, showing her scores when she first started keeping a record and then after three months.

	3 March	3 June
Life Overall	6	9
Joe Time	5	10
Children Time	8	10
Fitness	4	7
Balance	5	9
10s and Big Rocks	2	9
Friendships	3	8
Connection to God	10	10
Nutrition	4	7
Ideal Day	4	9
Meditation/Prayer	2	10
Fun vs. Drudgery	4	7
Reading/Learning	5	9
Community Work	1	7

The $16,000,000 Exercise

Next, I asked Sue to imagine that she won or inherited $16,000,000 tax-free. I asked her, "Would your mother be critical of that?" "No," she responded, "Because that would just be good luck." In working with poor boy/girl I find that this belief is typical. It's okay to win or be given money; it's just not all right to earn it. I asked Sue to decide what she would keep the same now that she had all this money and what would she change. In this way she started to expand her view of life and imagine some new possibilities for herself.

Feeling Like a Millionaire

It was important for Sue to start experiencing what it felt like to actually enjoy the fact that she was now wealthy. Her homework required her to go to a jewelry shop and try on some pieces worth $20,000 or more. Then she was to go to some designer stores and try on new outfits. She was also to test drive expensive foreign cars. She was not to buy anything in any of these places. The purpose of the exercise was for Sue to pay special attention to how she felt as she did these things she had never considered doing before. It helped her identify some core beliefs that were possibly not serving her any more.

Sue found in this homework activity that her core belief of poor girl had become quite a mooring line. She found herself saying that she didn't deserve time away from the household work and she certainly didn't deserve to own clothing that was gorgeous and expensive. She also found herself saying no to some fun proposals from Joe, because she believed that the children should be the most important thing in their marriage and everything else, including time with her husband, should take second place. There was another old standby that she found herself admitting with a blush—that idle hands were the devil's tools.

Propellants

As Sue shared her responses to her wealth consciousness homework, she started to become aware that many of the attitudes she had been carrying around inside her were no longer relevant to her new lifestyle. It was time to find out what tools she could draw upon to encourage herself to move towards, rather than away from, the new life her husband was offering her. It was time to find some propellants that would move Sue in the direction she now felt she'd like to go.

As the name suggests, propellants are beliefs or attitudes that can propel us in a certain direction. They can include a whole range of emotions, both positive and negative, from beholdenness, love, appreciation, and adventure, to guilt, fear, greed, addiction or arrogance. It was fun exploring the possibilities with her, and she discovered that her main propellants were her love for Joe and her desire to make their marriage work. She also recognized that she had a huge desire to please, a strong sense of excellence, a real fear of failing, and a lifelong need for approval from her mother and father.

The Result

As Sue and Joe became adept in the Daily Accountability process, they learned they could actually grade how a day was going at any point in the day and make any needed adjustments straight away. They discovered that, as they shared their grades and their feelings, they were relating to each other in a new, much closer way. They began expressing the feelings they had simply shut down for a long time. Sue found herself telling Joe that she felt he often treated her like one of his employees. Joe responded by making a commitment to pay more attention to his communication with her. Needless to say, there were benefits to this that flowed into their sex life. The change this made to their intimacy certainly became a very positive propellant for him.

For Sue, life continues to expand. She has moved into a place of appreciation for the fact that she no longer has to keep within a tight budget. She is prepared to allow herself to enjoy the benefits of what her new life has to offer. She and Joe now have at least one date night a week when they employ a babysitter and take time out just for the two of them. Sue has also learned to set healthy boundaries with her children.

Exercise One

Daily Accountability Chart

We have been exploring ways of designing your own Magnificent Life, honoring aspects of life and living that hold particular value to you, such as health and fitness matters, business goals or spiritual practice.

Using the chart in Appendix 1 as a model, take time to design your own daily accountability chart by including elements that are important to you. Over the next week, check in with yourself morning and night and record the results. If your scores are low in any particular area, consider what mooring lines may be holding you back and what propellants you could engage to fulfill your commitment in that aspect of your life.

Exercise Two

Propellants

Take one of your goals and write a list of possible propellants you might use to assist you in achieving it. For example, if deadlines are a propellant that works for you, design some deadlines for taking the steps or fulfilling the commitments required for achieving your goal.

8

Wealth Consciousness

"The least of things with a meaning is worth more in life than the greatest of things without it." Carl Jung

Wealth and You

What is wealth? What comes to mind when I mention the word? How do you react in your body? Do you feel your breath deepening, your chest expanding? Is there a smile on your face? Or does the mere mention of the word make you shrink inside, while your body closes down? I suggest that you take note of your physiological reactions during your reading of this chapter as they may give you some insight into hidden beliefs within you about wealth and your relationship with it.

We live on a planet of great abundance. Everywhere in nature we see examples of how the Divine Creator provides abundance and plenty. Take the genus of insects known as Lepidoptera; this classification of the insect world encompasses 15,000 species of butterflies and more than 250,000 kinds of moths. If the Creator can design a world in which just one insect genus has so many varieties, imagine the wealth of opportunities and experiences out there waiting for us to discover them.

Yet so many of us cling to the belief of scarcity or lack—we believe that there are simply not enough resources in the world to go around.

Wealth

The word wealth conjures up many different layers of meaning. **Wealth to**

the Power of Three is my way of conceptualizing the elements that make up a balanced Magnificent Life.

Wealth 1

When you've achieved *Wealth 1*, you have developed a daily appreciation for the gift of life and are actively doing what it takes to have a 10 day, every day. A magnificent day would be characterized by true balance between personal, spiritual and emotional aspects of being and income-generating activities. (Appendix 1 provides a checklist you can use to see how you are doing in terms of genuinely nurturing your hopes, dreams, goals and aspirations in all aspects of your life.)

At this level, you consciously draw upon your skills to create meaning and joy on a daily basis in your life. This would include using tools such as 10s and 25s—giving and receiving these and being open to adding new ones to the list. You are attuned to your ideal day and ideal week and you have your own internal monitoring systems that let you know when you're getting off track.

When at work, you are exclusively Dollar-Productive and have strategies and skills to manage the constant distractions of people, events, technology and your own inner voices. In Wealth 1 you focus on the larger picture of balance which, since life is primary, includes time with family and friends, sports and nature as well as business. Material abundance is balanced by quality time with loved ones, friends, sporting interests and community activities.

For those parents, children and elders who are not engaged primarily in income generating, in your ideal day/week, you are expressing the externalization of your Unique Psychological Fingerprint. You are unfolding your own vision and destiny path in activities that most reflect who you are.

If you were to suddenly find out that you had a terminal illness, could you face your own mortality with a sense that you had achieved what was important to you, instead of being filled with regrets? Remember, I want you to have 50s and 75s at least once or twice every year before you die. After you die, you can't do the trips to Disneyland or climb Mt. Kilimanjaro. The rules change when you don't have a body.

I Wish ...

As a Rabbi I have been honored over the years to visit with, support and console many people on their deathbeds. When I ask these people what they remember most about their lives, they usually tell me things like sitting on their grandfather's knee as a child and listening to his stories, watching their mom make her special chicken soup, their dad taking them on their first driving lesson, the first time they met their beloved, celebrating their child's Bar Mitzvah and so on. In other words, the common theme is time spent with the special people in their lives doing special things.

It is notable then, that when people are preparing to leave this world, very few spare a thought for the time they spent at work. In fact, work is more often mentioned in terms of regret. "I wish I'd spent less time at work and more time with my family," is a refrain I have heard quite often. Instead of you looking back on your life and being filled with regret, get it right while you are still alive. Look at the things you can change now and how you might go about it.

I Should Have Told Her

When I was conducting a funeral in Cleveland, Ohio, the weather was freezing and snow covered the ground. As darkness fell, I became concerned as everyone else had gone and the widower was still standing by the snow-covered grave. He just kept staring at his wife's grave and muttering something, presumably to his deceased wife who had died of malignant breast cancer at the age of 41. The man was young too, around 44 years old and they had two children aged 14 and 9.

Finally, I went over to the widower, who was a scientist with NASA, and touched him on the shoulder. When he turned to me, I could see there were tears in his eyes.

"I should have told her," he said. "We were married for over 20 years and I never told her." I asked him what it was he should have told his now deceased spouse and his face was distraught as he replied, "I never told her how much I loved her."

This man's belief had been that his work was so important it superseded everything else. He believed his responsibilities as a husband and father were discharged if he provided his family with a comfortable lifestyle. The tragedy was that it took his wife's death to teach him how important it is to tell the people we care about how much they mean to us, daily.

I felt the tragedy of this man's situation. If he could have relived this time he would have made quite different choices. My message to you is simple: Don't wait until it is too late. If your relationship with wealth and work is not giving you the Magnificent Life you would love, make a conscious choice now, while you are working through this chapter, to change it.

Start Now

Towards the end of this chapter, you are invited to keep a time log—to keep an honest record of how you spend the minutes of your life both at work and at play, for a limited period of time. This can be a very revealing and sometimes humbling exercise that can help you to identify the real priorities you have consciously or unconsciously been observing in your daily life. You may be startled to discover how much time you've been devoting to busy work when at work and maybe how little attention you've been giving your beloveds or yourself when at home.

I believe that most of us desecrate the precious hours of our life, both in the workplace and in time off, when we fall unconscious and allow others, or our addictions, to take us over and divert us from our real purpose.

Wealth 2

This is the level that most people think of when considering the concept of wealth. Put bluntly, it's not only money in the bank, it's also, and more importantly, income that is earned and accumulates for you whether you go to work or not—passive income. This can include interest, dividends, rents and income from businesses you own and don't manage.

When you've achieved *Wealth 2*, you don't have to go to work. However, you may choose to because you love your career.

I offer this challenge every time I work with a group of people: "If you never went back to work again, what would your annual pre-tax income be? What would you like your annual pre-tax income to be for the rest of your life?"

The goal is to make the transition from just working and living off an earned income to being able to live off the dividends from your investments. This is the level where mastery of money is such that wealth is being created continually through assets such as property, stocks and bonds.

At level 2 wealth, you are well familiar with gross and net income, pension plans, tax shelters, living trusts, how to build an asset base and how to invest or supervise investments. I subscribe to the saying that "you don't have to be wealthy to invest, but you do need to invest to be wealthy"— unless you've inherited from someone who created the fortune for you. In the latter case, unless you have a strong enough character structure to resist the addiction to consuming, and a wise investment strategy is put in place along with income protection protocols, huge fortunes can disappear, almost magically, overnight.

There are many highly knowledgeable advisers available today to share their wisdom on the skills and techniques of investment. I do not claim to possess any particular skills or techniques in this area, and I recommend that you use your discretion and intuition to find the teacher or mentor most appropriate to your needs to guide you in this important area. My concern lies with what mooring lines are holding you back from taking the most necessary steps towards developing passive income and what might serve as propellants to inspire you to fulfill your commitments in this area.

What often fascinates me is the change that comes over a person's face when he tells me about how much he just made in a deal and then the glassy stare in their eyes when I ask, "How much of that income did you put away in an investment?" It is my belief that when we are paid for our work, we should make a commitment to pay ourselves first.

By that I don't mean run off and buy ourselves that fabulous car or outfit we've been admiring for months, but rather that we make a commitment to take at least 20% of our earnings each week or month and place this in an account earmarked for investment for passive income. Once you've taken the "sacred" 20% out—as your double tithe towards your future well-being—then you look at how you will disburse the rest of your active income for whatever obligations and/or dreams you'd like to fulfill. I encourage you to consider taking even just this one step and making it a habit for the rest of your life.

Wealth 3

Level 3 wealth manifests when we reach a level of understanding about how the world really works and our place in it. *Wealth 3* is about being on our own life path and being able to tell if we slip away from it and get lost. If we do get lost, we have the skills and awareness to find our way back within a few hours or days, not years.

Wealth 3 graduates combine a renaissance education with street savvy. At this level you have developed a philosophical system that gives your life meaning. You understand and are aligned with your destiny path. Wealth at this level is an inclusive wealth, where attributes such as wisdom, compassion, financial understanding, common sense, and political and social awareness blend to equip you as a true citizen of the world, both giving and receiving its gifts.

At *Wealth 3*, you're likely to have in place your own particular spiritual disciplines which help you to stay aligned with your purpose or destiny. At the same time, you are not naïve; your life will often take paths of continuing education where you update your skills in technological developments and human understanding in an ongoing way.

I like to describe this level as the "I know that I know" level. This is where you are no longer looking outside for direction in terms of your life's purpose, but are still aware of the necessity of consulting and seeking out information or guidance from others who may have more knowledge than you in particular areas. When receiving guidance, you are then able to tune in to your inner guidance system, or Inner Mastermind group, to assess how appropriate this information is to your own particular situation. This is the Black Belt stage.

The Work Ethic

It seems to me that people are being sold the notion that to simply turn up at work for a certain number of hours per day is the same as being worthwhile and productive. We are led to believe that there is some inherent goodness in work. Furthermore, advertising tells us that as long as we are earning money so that we can buy more consumer goods, we are doing everything that is required to lead a fulfilling life.

Has the work ethic in fact enslaved us? I believe that these messages are mind viruses; much like the viruses you get on your home computer. If they are left unchecked, they can grow, multiply and eventually take over and destroy all the healthy data and memory on your hard drive. Mind viruses have the same effect on the human brain. If they are not counteracted with healthy, life-supporting data, an individual can lapse into dejection and listlessness. It is my contention that individuals who are connected to their Tall Poppy essence can be trained to identify and counteract mind viruses, using antidotes such as the exercises in this book.

During World War II, Jewish prisoners at Auschwitz were mocked by a sign on the entrance to the camp that said, "Arbeit mach frei," which translated to English means, "Work makes you free." This was the ultimate cruel twist on the Nazi view of the work ethic.

In modern times, we are seeing the work ethic exerting an insidious power in another form. These days we have a new form of addiction that is called workaholism. For many it starts out as a way of survival and buying food, clothing and shelter. Then maybe it becomes a way of getting approval or fitting in. Then it just becomes the norm.

The point is that work, like everything else in life, must take its rightful place in a life constellation.

I have a favorite mantra that I like to share with people who suddenly realize how much of their life's energy is consumed by their work. "Life is primary and work funds life." It's not meant to be the other way round.

Please don't dedicate yourself to a lifestyle that will guarantee regrets. As Jung's quote reminds us, it is vital to identify who and what give our life meaning—the people we cherish and the 10s that make our hearts sing—and then our business and careers become the means by which we finance those desires.

Especially when we are doing what we love and enjoy and are stimulated by our work, we need to take responsibility for ensuring it is in balance with the rest of our life. Too often I have caught myself totally absorbed in a project or a sheet of investment earnings, which are a real fascination to me, and then looked up to see my wife or my son about to give up on the realization of the promised quality time together.

Money by Chance

Sometimes people come into sudden wealth without having any developed wealth consciousness. Examples of this include athletes who are propelled into lucrative salary or sponsorship deals, actors who suddenly find themselves "hot properties," able to command big paychecks, and people who win the lottery. If there is not an infrastructure or honorable role models and a support system in place, these lucky people don't know how to deal with their sudden influx of wealth. They may even ignore it. I heard about one lottery winner, a fry chef in a local greasy spoon, who didn't know how to tell his friends and family that he had won a heap of money so he simply continued at his old job, even traveling to work each day on the bus.

I sometimes watch with dismay when wealthy and successful parents (who are often trying to compensate for the fact that they are seldom home) think they are doing their children a favor when they indulge them with money and gifts. These parents think that what they are doing is an act of love, but often they can be creating energetic stumbling blocks that will prevent their evolving offspring from developing their own respect for the energy called money. I see it as a way of destroying the child's will and sense of achievement. I believe an important role of parents is to train their children in wealth consciousness. This will provide them with the skill set to live life as an adventure, with part of that adventure being the accumulation of abundance. I would prefer that parents spend their children's inheritance.

It is my observation that when people have not prepared themselves to deal wisely with money, they sometimes find themselves unable to cope with it and so they may divest themselves of it as quickly as possible. The rags to riches story can certainly happen in reverse. Unwise investments, a heady lifestyle, trusting an untrustworthy advisor; we have all heard the stories of what can happen when there is no appreciation of the role of money and how it can evaporate as quickly as it appeared. How easy it is to become a slave to consumer debt through credit-funded purchases.

I believe that our obligation to our Soul is to create wealth to support our dreams rather than curtail them because of a limited budget. Instead of settling for living off social security at retirement and shrinking your life accordingly, why not look for greater and greater expansion, new opportunities and challenges?

So let's explore the practical aspects of a wealth creation. You could say that the Wealth to the Power of Three principles represent the theory, now let's look at how to actually manifest your desire to increase your income and fund your Magnificent Life.

Here's a little story to start with ...

A Hard Day's Work

Mandy is a realtor who has been in the industry for five years. She works in a medium-sized office that is owner-operated and employs three other salespeople besides her. It is located in a middle-class suburb of predominantly family homes. Mandy's office competes for listings with two highly visible real estate offices and several other moderately active ones, like Mandy's.

On this particular day as Mandy climbs in her car to drive home from work, she feels exhausted. As she drives, she mentally ticks off the things she has achieved in the previous eight hours. First thing she did when she arrived at the office that morning was return half a dozen phone messages. As a result, some of the appointments she thought were confirmed for today were actually re-scheduled. With the day suddenly looking clearer, she had made some further inquiries about the sales conference planned for next month that she's been given the job of organizing. At least she finally has the venue sorted out now and she's started to compile a short list of potential caterers. Then she had lunch with some of the other sales staff at that new restaurant everyone's been dying to try. That went on a bit long, but it was fun. After that, the afternoon was pretty much wasted but she did manage some paperwork, followed by some more emails, then she confirmed her appointments for tomorrow. Finally, before calling it a day, she tidied up the clutter on her desk so everything would be ready and waiting for tomorrow.

All in all, it was a very productive day. Or was it?

Busy Work and Dollar-Productive Behavior

A very important distinction needs to be made here. For salespeople like Mandy whose income is based mainly on commission, there is a vast difference between Dollar-Productive Activities and being busy.

Busy work is any activity that makes you look as if you are busy doing something when you're really just filling in time doing something a person on a basic wage could do. Dollar-productive activities are any activities that will produce income. If we analyze the day's work described above, Mandy spent valuable, potentially dollar-productive time doing tasks such as confirming appointments, organizing a sales conference, and tidying up her desk, which could have been delegated to a personal assistant being paid an hourly rate of $10 to $15.

For Mandy, as a real estate salesperson, there are four primary activities that would qualify as dollar-productive for her: prospecting, listing, negotiating, and selling and keeping a deal together. She didn't touch any of these elements in her hard day's work. Indeed, one of the easiest ways to discover what dollar-productive behavior is, is to identify those behaviors that are NOT. Often workshop participants proudly tell me how they are turning over millions of dollars in sales each year and that they still put up their own For Sale signs. They even take all the photographs for their marketing campaigns. To me this is the work ethic gone wrong. They are effectively using potentially highly dollar-productive hours to do administrative tasks that could be delegated to someone else.

If you are an entrepreneur, a person making your living through commission on product sales or through the sale of your time, I would be willing to bet that at present, you are doing a maximum of 8 dollar-productive hours of work a week. I can hear you protest, because last week you put in a 60-hour week and you never got to see your son playing in that important rugby or soccer match. I invite you to consider a way to double your dollar-productive hours. How would it be to go from 8 to 16 hours of dollar productivity and instead of doing this in 60 hours—doing it in 20 to 30 hours? You could work Monday to Wednesday and take the rest of the week off. Take a deep breath and just bear with me for a moment. The key to this work is breathtakingly simple—as long as you are willing to spend a few minutes a day on the exercise below.

Time Log

If you are serious about designing your own Magnificent Life, through increasing your income levels and freeing up time, try this exercise. Take out your diary or personal planner and begin to list the activities you engaged in at work today, at 15-minute intervals. Include the phone calls you made, the administrative work including that photocopying you did, the trip to the car wash, the letters you wrote, the time spent checking emails and the chats with your coworkers.

Repeat this exercise every day for the next two weeks. When the time is up, go back and look at your records. For every activity you did that will produce income, either immediately or in the future, put a dollar sign beside it. Be honest because this is for your own benefit. You may have some startling and uncomfortable revelations about how you have been passing your time during this period, perhaps even kidding yourself that certain activities that you called work were actually only busy activities. Did you make valuable connections at the networking breakfast you attended or did you just talk to the friend you went with? Did that two-hour slot last Thursday that you spent calling past clients generate any strong leads? How much time can you devote to doing the same thing this week?

When you have completed the exercise, take a moment or two to process what you have learned about the way you work. Could you readily identify which activities will actually produce money for you? Can you see some ways you can increase your dollar productivity during the hours you are at work? Look at those activities next to which you have put a dollar sign. Do they fill the working hours of each day or are they spread out over five or six days in the week you just recorded? Did you identify time spent on potential investments and the likely rate of return? Are you at the stage where the only debt you are prepared to take on is asset-building debt such as mortgage payments on investment properties?

What would happen if you redesigned your ideal week so that you are committed to performing the Dollar-Productive Activities you've identified in three days rather than six? What would you do with the other days? More time with your family? Golfing with friends or clients? I have clients who work only three days a week at triple their former income. Just think of the Magnificent Life you could design for yourself if you had triple your current income as well as several extra days a week in which to enjoy your 10s.

What support, if any, will you need to put strategies in place to create new work habits? How would you like to spend any time away from work that you might be able to enjoy once you are earning more money?

Make the Commitment

It's that simple. We've talked earlier about goals and commitments and an Eight Point Plan. If the idea of doubling your dollar-productive hours at work and doing these in three or four days, instead of five or six, has appeal to you, then it's time to put your theory into practice.

Write down your commitment to do X number of dollar-productive hours in X number of days. Write down what those activities are and when you will do them. What do you need to put in place to assist you, to remove any potential mooring lines to your success and what propellants would help inspire you to act? What rewards and non-rewards will you put in place? Who will hold you accountable? Involve your peer partner in this process and do some brainstorming on what else you might need to consider or put in place to ensure your success. Use the Sample Ideal Day sheet in Appendix 5 and Exercises Two and Four at the end of this chapter.

Now, there's one more element I'd like to share with you to put in place the activities that will move you towards your wealth creation goals. This is the more intangible aspect of Wealth Consciousness, and one that I've found immensely important.

Morning Ritual

This is the food with which I start my day, which nourishes and supports me throughout the rest of the day.

Many years ago I began the practice of starting my day with time set aside for me and my Soul. I have referred to this briefly earlier in the book. My morning ritual usually begins at 5 or 5:30am and, depending on how much time I allow myself, can take anywhere from 20 minutes to 2 hours to complete.

The practice begins with a period of stretching exercises, paying attention to the Temple of my body and allowing my body to heal itself through being gently challenged and worked out. I will then take time to sit quietly and meditate. I sit in my favorite old chair and allow my breath to open me and take me where my Soul wants me to go. Sometimes this practice takes 15 to 20 minutes, sometimes 2 minutes. Whatever the length of time, I come out of this feeling clear and refreshed. Either at the beginning or the end of the meditation time, I will set my intention for the day ahead for who I want to be during my day.

Whether it is to be a day of teaching a group, or doing coaching on the telephone, or a day with the family, my intention will be shaped to fit my desire to be of the most service and to come from a clear and pure heart. If I have particular financial concerns or goals, then I may set an intention specific to this as well and ask for guidance on the best practice to observe in this area.

Next, a rigorous walk with my wife is one of my favorite ingredients of the morning ritual. It gives us a chance to catch up with each other, to talk about dreams we had the night before and to discuss our plans for the day ahead.

On return home, the morning ritual includes bathing, followed by choosing the colors and clothes I feel called to wear that day. When you go to choose your clothes tomorrow, do pay attention to how you feel when you put an item of clothing on. If you don't feel quite right in it, then change it and let your intuition choose the colors and styles that most support and reflect who you are for the day.

The last part of my morning ritual is the grinding of coffee and the preparation and true enjoyment of my favorite beverage. I'm ready for the day. As I mentioned above, if for some reason I do not perform my morning ritual, I often find that I bump my way through the day, perhaps saying things I later regret, or forgetting to do things that were important to me. When I become aware of what's happening at these times, it is a reminder to me of just how powerful the One-Mindedness that comes from a daily spiritual practice is and how nourishing it has become for me.

And Finally, a Bit of Philosophy

There is a simple truth in nature that we can apply to the modern work ethic. A queen bee, as you probably know, is the only fertile female within a bee colony. She is responsible for maintaining a strong population of worker bees; although once her offspring are produced, she takes no further responsibility for them.

In bee farming, the queen is replaced regularly to ensure a thriving colony. The fascinating point to note here is that female larvae destined to be queen bees are no different physically or genetically from larvae destined to be worker bees. The only difference is the food they are fed. Larvae chosen to be queen bees are fed royal jelly for the entire larval stage. Enough royal jelly is then absorbed into the bee's body to stimulate production of the royal pollen. She is then the newly anointed queen.

If we apply the metaphor of designer queen bees to Tall Poppies, we can say that they have both been fed differently. The queen bee has achieved her status passively; that is, she was fed the royal jelly by her minders. For us, angels in human form, we need to play a more active role in paying attention to how we feed our body, mind and soul.

The kind of food I'm talking about can take many different forms—from the newspapers or magazines we read, to the television programs or movies we watch, to the kind of people we hang out with on a regular basis. All of these elements of our life that we may have taken for granted can exert both positive and negative influences on who we are and the quality of our life. The spoken or written word can be one of the most nourishing or damaging types of food we take in. The next time you pick up a newspaper that has photos of the latest human carnage or even a celebrity marriage break-up on the cover, pay attention to any changes you feel. A few minutes ago you may have been feeling quite calm and at peace within. How do you feel now as you read about another suicide bombing in Iraq or Israel? Do you feel any tightness in your stomach?

I have restricted my reading of the newspaper to once or twice a week for my update on what's been happening in the world. Apart from sending prayers to victims of violence and injustice, I feel there is probably little I can do to change the situation of those poor souls on the cover of the paper. However, I do know that I can change my own situation and also be of help to those with whom I choose to associate every day. I know that I can feed my Soul and start my day in peace by reading from books that are sacred to me. By telling my beloved how much I love her or by thanking my assistant for a particularly fine job done, I can positively impact their days too.

So, how are you feeding yourself as you move through your day? Do you start your day reading the daily doom and gloom reports or do you take time to meditate or listen to an educational CD of some kind? Do you hang out with people who are negative and complaining or do you seek out friends who uplift your spirits each time you see them? Do you spend your lunch hour eating a sandwich at your desk, or do you take the time to go out and walk through the nearby park? In her groundbreaking research into amino acids called neuropeptides, Candace Pert discovered a direct link between external events and the molecular functioning of our bodies. Her fascinating book, *Molecules of Emotion*, is well worth reading. She discovered that watching a violent movie, for example, can throw our internal organs out of balance, sometimes for many days, as the neuropeptides take time to recover from the shock of witnessing pain and hearing loud noise.

Sometimes, the food we need to help us make changes in our lives can come in the form of an abrupt wake-up transformational experience. This can be something we didn't consciously choose. Anything from divorce to redundancy can push us into reviewing our lives and our values and into investigating alternative ways of seeing the world. At times of crisis we are often catapulted into seeking out a different frame of reference for this new state in which we find ourselves.

Answers may come through therapy, self-development books and courses or trying out different spiritual practices. One thing that has impressed me over the years as I have checked in with friends and clients whose souls used the more cathartic means of getting their attention, not one of them has said that they would prefer to go back to the way they were before they had the wake-up call. Every one expressed appreciation for how they were able to get to the point in their lives of acknowledging that the experience was in some way necessary and strangely beneficial, especially in prompting them to take more responsibility for their own lives.

Unlike the worker bees who never have a choice over whether or not they become Queens because it is simply a matter of random selection, Tall Poppies are people who in some way or another, have chosen to take on the mantle of their Divine essence. In so doing, you assume responsibility for doing what it takes to achieve what you want and to live a life that holds meaning and purpose for you.

Exercise One

Getting Clear

Using the information you have gathered in your time log, it is time to make some decisions. Take four different colored pens and design a code for your present activities. The code might be something like this:

1. Purple—busy work activities I can delegate.
2. Green—dollar-productive activities I wish to keep and/or do more of.
3. Red—desecration activities I need to eliminate.
4. Orange—inspired new activities I want to incorporate into my day/week.

Return to your time log and mark the activities shown there according to where they fit in your new code. With the orange pen, write a list of the activities you want to incorporate into your Ideal Day and Ideal Week.

Note: If you are a person who is not engaged in traditional income-earning work, please fill out this log replacing the section for dollar-productive activities with a description that fits the activity that holds the highest value or priority for you. This may be Soul Time or Family Time or Writing Time—tune in to your inner voice and pay attention to what words or expressions come through to you in this exercise.

Exercise Two

Dollar-Productive Behavior and Things I Will No Longer Do

It's time now to get specific and really focus on the activities you know you need to do more of in your business and also those you need to dispense with. Take out Appendices 2 and 3 and get to work!

Exercise Three

Ideal Day

You can download copies of all the appendices online at www.drfredgrosse. com. Doing so will make it easier to work with each sheet.

Make seven copies of the Ideal Day sheet noted in Appendix 5.

Begin by designing your Ideal Day. You can refer to the Sample Day Sheet in Appendix 4 before you get started and check inside to see what elements you'd like to include. For this exercise, in addition to being clear about the dollar-productive activities you want to plan, really listen to the yearnings of your soul and see what elements you could add to the activities to create a day that makes your heart sing. If you like, use the colored pens to highlight the dollar-productive and inspired new activities you are incorporating into your schedule.

Please remember—dollar-productive hours must be balanced with time set aside for your health, your relationships, your spiritual life and play time.

Exercise Four

Ideal Week

Do the same process that you did in Exercise Two but this time fill out a sheet for each day of the week. Be specific about the time allocations you make. For example, on Mondays you might include swimming 7 to 7:30am, calling clients 9:30 to 11:30am, checking investments 3 to 4pm, and massage 6 to 7pm. Tuesdays, you might like to start the day with a walk with a friend, and so on.

9

Sacred Living

*"The meeting of two personalities is like the
contact of two chemical substances: if there is
any reaction both are transformed." Carl Jung*

Sacred Community

One of the greatest pleasures in my work is to witness what I call the
alchemical reactions between people in the groups. I have come to understand and appreciate that while it may have been peoples' intellects or
business concerns that prompted them to pick up the phone and call my
office to sign up for a seminar, it was their Souls that moved them to pay
attention in the first place. In the first few minutes of participants taking their seats in the room and looking around them, often nervously, to
see who else is there, I begin to sense the connections that already exist
between people, even though they haven't yet made their acquaintance.

By the end of the first two days together, it is not unusual for people to
announce in amazement that they feel like they've known X and Y all their
lives or that someone just happened to say something that totally reso-
nated for them and made them rethink where they were in their own life.
It has become clear to me that there are no chance encounters and that in
group or community work, in particular, certain souls have made a commitment to be there for each other and to assist the other in their development. This is the case even when two people appear to be in disagreement
and dislike each other.

143

Often, years into a program, I've observed two individuals who may have spent their first sessions studiously avoiding each other, finally getting to the point where they could communicate their mistrust or reservations. In so doing, they found a whole new perspective suddenly opening up, usually on themselves. From then on, the two opponents become allies, often with a deep sense of respect for each other.

Any contact with another human being, however fleeting, has the potential to be transformative for both parties. As Jung says, this transformation can be as explosive as the mixing of two chemical substances like hydrogen and nitrogen and the results can be either positive or negative. If you smile at the man who runs the corner store when you buy your bread and eggs and engage him in conversation, you are offering him a gift that could potentially transform his day. Likewise, if you snarl at him for keeping you waiting or complain about how expensive his canned spaghetti is then his experience of you is likely to cast a shadow over his day. He might react with a sarcastic comment and thereby confirm your belief that he isn't a nice person.

Next time someone cuts you off on the freeway, pay attention to what happens in your body, to any tightening you feel in your stomach or shoulders. Then take a deep breath and see if there is anyone around you for whom you could make room. As they wave in gratitude to you for letting them into your lane, see how that makes you feel inside. In a few minutes you're likely to see this person offering the same courtesy to someone else up ahead in traffic and maybe you feel a warmth at the mushroom effect your one act of kindness is having. We have choices available to us every few seconds in life, and we can choose to get stuck in reactivity, victim mode or anger, or we can choose to turn the energy into something positive and life-affirming, such as bringing our own touch of kindness to the freeways of life.

We all have the power to contribute to the well-being, or otherwise, of the people around us, whether in the intimacy of the family circle, or the wider community of our workplace, the local shopping mall or our church, synagogue or mosque. When we gather with a commonality of purpose, we can create what I call sacred communities, where common values and ideals can form a bond and where lifelong friendships and commitments to each other's well-being are simply accepted as the norm.

What excites me is the idea of a world where people can create sacred communities of like-minded individuals where we can share our successes, our challenges, unscramble things and be mutually supportive in a trustworthy way. These networks have a wonderful way of just evolving. As one person shines his or her light in a beloved relationship, family, workplace, church or neighborhood, others want to know how he did it. Much like the woman in the restaurant in the movie *When Harry Met Sally*, they say, "I'll have what she's having," and so the movement grows.

Sacredness

The Oxford Dictionary defines sacred as "consecrated or held dear to a deity, hallowed by religious association or tradition, inviolable."

Take a moment now and just tune in to the energy of the word sacred for yourself. What comes to mind for you?

For me, I find myself transported to the Grand Canyon and the sense of awe I experienced the very first time I beheld nature's work there. As I hiked down to the base of the Canyon, I felt myself very protective of the rocks, the scant vegetation and even the snakes of which I caught glimpses. This place, for me, had sanctity and I felt personally violated when I came across trash that other hikers had left behind. When I climbed up Mount Sinai with my son David at daybreak in June 1979, for his Bar Mitzvah, it was a sacred moment for me. This is the mountain declared sacred by Moses.

A fine cup of Sulawesi Kalossi coffee early in the morning while I'm outside watching the ducks gobble Fred's Bread is a sacred moment for me. I find myself absolutely fully present and touched by the focus of these beautiful birds as they make sure they get to every last crumb on the lawn.

Traditionally, the Sabbath is a day in the week that is set aside primarily to allow for a connection to the divine. We labor for six days and then on the seventh we rest and enjoy heaven on earth. Most religious traditions have provision for one sacred day each week. The rest of the week is, for most people, dedicated to more secular pursuits, such as earning a living.

So, when I talk about sacred community, sacred moments, sacred places, sacred relationships, I'm acknowledging the sense of deep connection, respect and even awe at the power of the moment or place. There is certainly a different energy that comes into play when we move to this level of attention. I believe that we, as individuals and also as members of collectives, can do much to transform places, situations and relationships by bringing an awareness of the sacred to these areas, events and gatherings.

Indeed, through ritual and intention, any place, any occasion can be made sacred. In a marriage ceremony, a relationship is made sacred. Magic moments can turn the ordinary into the sacred, when you find yourself feeling good and connected suddenly to a higher purpose. One of the outcomes of this level of awareness is usually a commitment to protect whatever it is that is held sacred. So let's look at some other areas in our lives where this can have meaning.

Sacred Relationships

As you may have gathered, I consider that our primary relationship, while we are in human form, is with our Soul. Our connection with our Soul represents our connection to the Divine. As in the martial arts, when your Soul works for you and with you, you have Black Belt status. You have the power of 10. In business, you can tell if your Soul is your ally, because you find yourself doubling your income every year.

If you're not doing so, it may be time for reflection. Have you disowned your Soul, or does your Soul want you to move in another direction? If you are an entrepreneur and you're fighting yourself—you'll sit down at your telephone to make prospecting calls and there you are reading the newspaper—to me that means your Soul has left. And that can become very expensive.

However, if you were to make a commitment along the lines of "this call is for my son's education, this one is for mother's surgery, this one is for taking the kids to Disneyland"—what impact do you think this would have on your calls and the energy you put into being of service in your work? That inner conflict that had been keeping you from doing what you knew you needed to do is most likely to dissolve. You're not fighting your desires any more—all of you is heading in the same direction, with a sense of purpose, imbued with the sacred.

Similarly, in your connections with other human beings in your work or business, pay attention to the thoughts and feelings you have for these individuals. If you're a commission salesperson and you are more worried about paying this month's mortgage payment than whether the product you're promoting is the most appropriate for your client, check how many deals you actually close.

Take a moment, before your next appointment, to hold the name of your prospective client in your heart and see him or her as another angel in human form sent to you for a purpose, one of which is for you to be of true service to him or her. Think of this person with loving kindness and send him or her a blessing of some kind before you actually come face to face. When you're with your client, pay attention to the quality of your interaction with this person and your own energy level as you seek to determine what they need the most. You may find yourself completely forgetting your own troubles and fully focusing on this Soul before you. The fact that they've just signed a contract may become less impactful than the knowingness that you have just helped this person find the house, the car, the vacuum cleaner that is absolutely the right one for them. And this may be the beginning of a lifetime relationship, whose nature you are committed to nurturing and protecting.

In the Jewish wedding ceremony, the vows between the man and woman are declared *kadosh*—sacred, and that word is repeated three times. The three time repetition makes it even more holy. In Jewish tradition, husband and wife are enjoined to honor their union as sacred, inviolable. The ancient law also provides for a release from this obligation, should the relationship lose this energy and the mutual commitment to its protection. Why stay in a relationship where you feel you are desecrating your Soul each time you are together?

Victoria and I have been married 18 years. At times it's a honeymoon relationship and at other times it's a classic battle of the sexes. What we both know is that we come from the same commitment to our relationship as a sacred ground, wherein we commit to support each other in our growth and fulfillment. If I come to our relationship when I'm not at one with my Soul, then I come to her out of sorts, out of focus. She doesn't get me, she gets part of me.

This will always be a work in progress and, if it no longer feels like one, then we need to sit down and assess our marriage. So often in the work I do with couples, I see a situation where there are no more beloveds, simply a campout situation where you come home, crash and refuel, change your oil and then go out again. Both souls in the relationship are stopping the flow of intimacy and opting for automatic mode. When I observe couples in this kind of rut, if I have a mandate to work with them, my first homework is for them to take a weekend together of giving each other 10s, being willing to both give and receive and to share the impact with each other. I will also ask them to do an additional time log, with special attention to what, if any, time they had been consecrating to being just with each other, with no other distractions.

In many households the television and the computer have become the gods. What I ask you to do, is bring your awareness to how you have allowed your days and weeks to shape themselves. Is it time, right now, to be proactive again and commit to a new Ideal Week that has time set aside to honor and enjoy your beloved?

If you have children, I'd ask you to do the same exercise. Take a moment to review the last time you gave your child your undivided attention. When did you last make sure you gave your son or daughter a few 10s? Did you allow your pager to interrupt your son telling you about the goal he hit this afternoon? If so, can you still see the crestfallen look on his face when you took out your cell phone and called that client?

Beloveds

You've seen me use this term often. I like this word. I find that when I use it to describe my beloved, I feel myself pausing and enjoying a warm glow around my heart. To me, my beloved is the one with whom I choose to spend my life. The one with whom I want to make major decisions and plan my 50s and 100s.

Being in a relationship with my beloved, I find myself both feeling cared for and wanting to care for her. This is a sense of genuinely wanting to be with her, rather than being together out of a sense of duty. We add to each other, want to make sure that what we plan is OK with the other and essentially see our roles as to help each other's unfolding as well as our own.

I know that many of you are not presently in relationship with a beloved. You may, however, be ready for one and perhaps actively looking. At times I find myself tuning into the Sufi mystics whose poems to the Beloved were actually love songs to the Divine. And so I encourage you to nourish the primary relationship you have with your Soul.

In so doing, you will find yourself tuning in to the Soul, the divine aspects of many other beings waiting to be touched and acknowledged. Animals such as dogs, horses and cats, easily respond at the soul level when they are in the presence of a human in contact at this level. You will find other people actually start to look different, to even glow, when you open yourself to see with the eyes of the heart. And, as you feel yourself relaxing into this new way of approaching people, expect the unexpected.

Sacred Selfishness

To juxtapose the word selfish with sacredness seems, at first glance, somewhat startling, if not downright confusing or contradictory terminology. Dr. Bud Harris, who is a Jungian psychologist, first coined the phrase *Sacred Selfishness* in his book of the same name. He defined it as valuing ourselves enough to be authentic human beings who give back vitality and hope to the people around us.

The dictionary defines selfishness as "deficient in consideration of others, actuated by self-interest." From tiny toddlers we are taught by our parents not to be selfish. We are told to share our toys with other children even when we want to play with that particular doll or ball or bike ourselves. It is seen as a necessary prerequisite, and of course, in many ways it is, to living in communities with others.

The problem arises, however, when children are not taught healthy boundaries around selfishness and sharing. In other words, many are taught a core belief to be self-sacrificing to the point where they put their own needs last, after everyone else. This taken to extremes can result in very unhappy adults who are experts at looking after everyone else—and don't know how to take care of themselves.

Just because your best friend calls you on the telephone to tell you about her latest fight with her boyfriend, do you need to set aside your plan to go to that play you had wanted to see? Then there is your co-worker who constantly comes into your office to get advice about how she should handle her clients, using up valuable time when you could be making sales calls. How does it help if we run ourselves ragged looking after others to the potential detriment of our own careers, personal lives and health?

It is important to realize that every time you say yes to something, you are also saying no to someone or something else. For instance, if I say yes to the colleague who needs my attention, I will be saying no to leaving early to have some private time with my beloved or my relaxation, exercise or meditation time, all of which are very important to me.

I believe that our primary responsibility is to our sacred selves. Therefore, I consult with my Inner Mastermind Group before I commit to other people's agendas. Working with my ideal day, week and fortnight means that when I have scheduled into my program that this hour is to be spent making coaching calls and tonight I'm seeing a play that has received rave reviews, then if someone else tries to claim that time for something else, I don't feel obligated to drop everything for them.

At the same time, I stay open and trust that my intuition will alert me to when I need to make an exception to this rule. From time to time a situation will arise in which a person may try to disguise a critical personal emergency as a mere request for advice and I have deeply regretted it when I didn't listen to that inner voice telling me to stop and pay attention to this one.

Sacred selfishness means making time for oneself, without the guilt of childhood conditioning, without being confluent with other people's rules. Our mission is to create a life that's worthwhile, and this is "our" life, rather than someone else's. Part of the adventure is that of harmonizing who we are with the culture of which we're a part. As we develop our ability to tune in to the Divine, like a global positioning system, we develop our own life and at the same time, we know we are never alone.

Noblesse Oblige

Like Dr. Bud Harris, I have worked with many clients who have taken the idea of selflessness to mean that they should always be looking after the needs of others and somehow ignore their own.

We saw this in the case study of Sue, whose tribal training was very strong. She had been taught since childhood to put the needs of others first. She had little or no relationship with her Soul and her relationship with her husband was under severe duress. Like a car without gas, she was running on empty, her days dedicated to the demands of her children and relatives. This was how Sue measured her self-worth and she had reached the point where she found herself severely wanting.

The French have an expression that reverses the pattern of what we saw in Sue's definition of service. The words *noblesse oblige* translate literally as nobility obliges—meaning that when you are in a privileged position, it is your obligation to extend help to others, to give back. I know that when I am tired and in need of a break from responsibilities, the level of service that I can extend to others is greatly reduced in effectiveness. For me to really perform at my best, I know that I must first ensure that I'm in good shape, physically, mentally and emotionally. It is my duty to look after myself so that I may then give my very best to others.

This brings me back to my starting point of the importance of one's relationship with the Soul and being in tune with that for which the Soul calls. When I am rested and refreshed, I want to give back. When I live according to noblesse oblige, my job is to live in my own authenticity and then to teach others to live in theirs and in so doing, to leave the world a better place.

Exercise One

Sacred Selfishness

Share the concept of sacred selfishness with two or three other people in your life network (family, friends, and colleagues) and just observe how they respond.

Exercise Two

Inner Mastermind Group

Call a meeting of your Inner Mastermind Group (your dominant, advisory sub-personalities) and discuss the concepts of sacred selfishness and sacred community with them. What objections does each sub-personality raise? List up to five objections from each. For example your Pleaser might protest—wondering what people will say.

Exercise Three

Imagine the Shoe on the Other Foot

Part A

Imagine someone who is honoring his or her sacred selfishness. For instance, they are on holiday with their family and you want to talk business with them. They say, "I'm sorry, I'm on holiday and this is precious time with my wife and children. How about we do this when I'm back in the office?" This doesn't suit you because you have time right now and the matter seems pressing to you. How do you react?

Part B

Now put yourself in their place. Perhaps it is your boss or manager or even a family member interrupting a moment you had set aside for yourself. Use your new understandings to write an imaginary script for responding to this person in which you honor sacred selfishness and show your respect for this person.

Exercise Four

Sacred Community

Visualize your ideal sacred community and name up to 10 people from your life right now who you would like to include in some way. What would be the foundations on which your relationships would be based? For example, it could include speaking the truth, respecting each other's goals, supporting each other in fulfilling commitments, etc.

10

Get a Life–A Magnificent One

*"The shoe that fits one person pinches another; there is
no recipe for living that suits all cases." Carl Jung*

Some years ago I was flying between Sydney and Melbourne, Australia,
and my attention was captured by a delightful mini movie by the mys-
tical Australian cartoonist, Leunig. In this slice of life, a morose-looking
character is walking around and his family and friends and others in the
street are sneering at him and telling him to get a life. Lost and confused,
his face lights up when he goes past a shop window advertising life for
sale. So, in he goes, only to discover that the lives for sale come in different sizes, in shoeboxes and they don't have his size. He tries on different
lives like shoes and does everything to contort himself this way and that
to fit in with what's available—to no avail. My heart still feels the impact
this made on me at the time as I tune in again to those images. So many of
us are doing just that—living someone else's life rather than our own, and
wondering what's missing, what's wrong, how come it just doesn't seem
to fit right?

As I said before, we came to this planet as incarnate angels and each
of us has a Unique Psychological Fingerprint with hopes, dreams, gifts and
talents that are specific to us as individuals. We each came with a mission,
a destiny to fulfill. We came here with imperfections, and we have work to
do to go to the next level, as I call it, before we are called home.

Just as in our garden we might prune a rose bush to give it shape and
vigor, just as a farmer will plow a field and add fertilizer before sowing the
crop seeds—so we too are continually called to work on ourselves for the
purpose of refining who we are. It is my firm belief that part of our respon-

sibility to ourselves and others is to align with our inner purpose and to externalize our dreams.

As we connect with what I call the three levels of wealth, we may find there are aspects of our understandings that we are called upon to share with others to help them develop their own inner resources. This is another way of reclaiming our Unique Psychological Fingerprint and putting it into the material world for the common good.

Are you ready to share your sense of inner power from a place of strength and compassion and to move on your path? At times you'll feel like a lone prophet contending with a Small Poppy collective. However, if you're willing to keep going, you will find there are many out there like you longing to form their own collective that reflects your worldview of incarnate angels.

Life Is Not a Dress Rehearsal

This catchy phrase has long appealed to me as a kind of wake-up call.

As I look around me, I see many people waiting to die, hallucinating in front of television or through mind-altering substances and keeping themselves on hold with no real purpose, waiting for something to happen. I feel great sadness at this. Yes, claiming and living a Magnificent Life has a lot to do with identifying and then pursuing your personal passions. It's not about watching someone else have a good time. I'm asking you to come back from disowning your life. It's time to externalize your own UPF. This is an unfolding process, rather like jumping into a flowing river as opposed to a dam overflowing. If you feel like you're treading water, this passive approach can get you swept along like you are in floodwater with no control over your direction. I'm asking you to get a boat and paddle.

Many of us keep waiting for life to happen without any real participation. This is like the bridegroom standing at the window on his wedding night, while his wife waits for him in bed, because his mother told him this would be the most wonderful night of his life. Many people are standing at the window of their lives. So what to do? Use the tools in this book. Keep your journal of 10s and 25s and keep paying attention to what moves you. I would hope that you'd have five hundred or more 10s to draw from to ensure you enjoy 10s every day. Work on your goals and Big Rocks and the special things that make life important. Using the Daily Accountability list in Appendix 1, check daily where you are and then ask yourself what tools you can use to improve in the areas of your life where your scores are low. Now that you've reached this level of understanding, you can't abdicate your part of the equation.

Destiny Path

Many think of destiny as a destination and that you can identify it through your intellect. Others think of it as a career. Some believe that innate talents have to do with destiny. Indeed, your career and the gifts and skills you discover you hold may well be clues. When I worked as a biochemist, I discovered that I had a lot of talent in this area and yet it was boring to me. However, when I entered seminary for my Rabbinical training, this felt like an amazing step in the direction of my destiny. I was studying what gave people's lives meaning and a sense of purpose and I just knew that this was where I was meant to be.

To me destiny is a knowingness. In some ways it's like air traffic control talking to a pilot. In this case, you are the pilot and air traffic control is the creator of the universe—the provider of destinies. Destiny is put in our cradle as our birthright. I have buried people who never opened the package of their own destiny. Essentially they avoided their life. They may have had children, they may have worked hard and appeared to live a nice life—yet always they had a sense they had missed out on what they were meant to be doing.

Unlike Moses bringing the Ten Commandments down from Mount Sinai, Destiny doesn't have to be something big. Great people and their neighbors all have a destiny that is being called from them. It can be a pathway that you check on. On a daily basis, ask yourself the question, on a scale of 1 to 10, am I in line with my destiny path? Like a game of hot and cold you will begin to know when you're close, when you're on track.

Some days you will feel more in line than on other days and you'll want to figure out what made the difference.

Sometimes it may simply be that you've had a good night's sleep, or a good connection with your beloved. Other times you will know, however, that there's a difference in the quality of feeling. It may be that your destiny is to be a good mother or father or to create wealth and teach others how to do the same. It may be that you are to be of service to people in your community or in a foreign land. When we connect with even an inkling of our destiny, it can give us a powerful sense of purpose and meaning. There are many distractions to this process and many can be worthy opponents for us. Please find out what you're meant to be doing before you leave.

Someone once told a child: "I'll give you a dollar if you'll tell me where God is." The child replied: "I'll give you a dollar if you'll tell me where God isn't." God is everywhere. Clues to your destiny are everywhere. However, your part is to open the door and invite it in—paradoxically, if you don't open the door, it's likely not to intrude on you. Life may create challenges of which we can become victims, and whine and moan. If we're oblivious to destiny calling, it's then hard to make the adjustments that are being called from us.

Beginning, Middle and End

Everything has a beginning, a middle and an end. As I said earlier, the *use-by-date* is the time when we need to throw away or release something. It's the energy in something that has died. Cheese, yogurt, locations, jobs, and even relationships all have use-by-dates.

When I talk about beginnings, middles and ends, I know I like beginnings. Like puppies and kittens and the fresh inquisitiveness they bring to their environment, I make a point of looking for areas or projects where I can start all over again in something. I like the challenge of applying my financial, educational and other resources to new circumstances. To me the opposite is to retire and die early.

In a Small Poppy culture when the use-by-date of retirement comes, so many people face the divorce from their daily occupation almost as a death sentence and give up on life. I see this as an opportunity for another new beginning. Freedom from work means we can dedicate ourselves to further destiny and life purpose work. This can be a transformational opportunity and this is another reason why I encourage people to invest, while they are actively earning, so their passive income can fund this part of their destiny path.

So many people think their work is who they are and that when they retire they become a *nobody*. When you retire, if you haven't already, will you/do you have a clear sense of what you're meant to be doing as part of your divine process? This is big medicine and I applaud President Jimmy Carter for the outstanding example he and his wife Rosalyn have given us in terms of retirement as the door to further transformation and noblesse oblige.

Get-a-Life Weekend

There is one area however, where I would encourage you to explore the possibility of extending the use-by-dates—in relationships.

Every year my wife and I have at least one "get-a-life" weekend. We set two days aside for talking about us as a couple. We don't answer the phone and we don't make any plans to socialize with friends over this weekend. At this time we review our core relationship and explore what we did well together and individually, what we would like more of and in what areas do we need to do better.

Our goal is to have what we call a honeymoon relationship. Now this doesn't mean that we don't have our disagreements in the course of our daily lives together—we have plenty of them. However, at our get-a-life sessions we look at how we're doing and we renew our commitment to each other, through the good and the bad times.

We make plans for holidays and trips we'd both like to do, look at how we can have quality time with our respective parents and extended families and friends. We look at our individual continuing education needs and desires and how these can be fitted into our seminar schedule. We both come to this meeting time with our own agendas, and these can often include issues that we know the other won't necessarily like. At these times the ground rule is that we will speak our truth, not interrupt each other and know that whatever is said is not intended to be hurtful, but needs to be expressed.

Life's Lessons

In his inspirational book *Man's Search for Meaning*, Viktor Frankl shares his experience of horrifying years in a concentration camp in Germany. Incarcerated and facing possible death moment to moment, Frankl came to understand that while his captors could take everything he owned away from him, including his life, there was one thing they could not take from him and that was his soul. He watched his fellow inmates and how they struggled to survive, some stealing, some betraying others for a chance to live another day, and he found that the greatest source of sustenance was inside himself. He found that almost anything could be endured if he could find some meaning in it.

Mercifully, there are few of us these days who are faced with the life-threatening types of circumstances that Frankl had to come to terms with. And yet, on a daily basis, Life presents us with situations and challenges that can throw us off balance and often into great turmoil. I call these Life Lessons and believe that such experiences are all part of our curriculum. We have all known some form of such experiences. Threatening strangers, rejections, betrayals, divorce, accidents, crippling illness—these all can be part of it.

This curriculum comes from another source—our job is to seek the lesson and to master it. Often people don't like the curriculum and rebel—like the prophet Jonah. According to the Scriptures, Jonah rebelled from going to Ninevah to tell the citizens there that they had to repent, and he ran away. Of course, his curriculum followed him. He took a boat to flee and in the midst of stormy seas he was thrown overboard and swallowed by a whale. This whale then spat him out on the shore and he was told to go about delivering his message to Ninevah.

Like Jonah, you're likely to find that if you try to deny or disown parts of yourself or your life path they will find you anyway. Like Frankl or Judas and the role he was called to play in betraying Jesus of Nazareth, our life challenges may sometimes be painful and even abhorrent. Our mission is to maintain a level of awareness in which we can ask ourselves, "What must I learn from this—and how?" The deeper challenge is often to resist the temptation to fall into victim or rebel consciousness and to open ourselves to learn how to master what's provided. In my view, there is no right or wrong in the curriculum—it is yours/ours.

If you try to live anyone else's curriculum, you're going to miss your own life. Keep asking yourself on a daily basis, "Am I on target with my life?" We're aiming for a 10 out of 10 score, even, indeed especially, when things are looking black. Pay attention, and when you score yourself at less than 10 with your curriculum, ask yourself, "How can I master what is being presented to me?" Whether it's a tax lien, a lawsuit, a sick child, elderly parents—whatever the challenge is, you have a chance to become a Black Belt or a victim.

For many of us the reflex reaction is often to use excuses rather than solutions, to use the Whiner sub-personality rather than the Problem Solver. At times like this, bring your consciousness in to work for and with you. Call upon your Wise Person and your Inner Teacher to guide and strengthen you. When you take on your Black Belt energy in this way and answer the call of your curriculum, you have access to an immense source of power and wisdom, and the Force is with you.

Your Magnificent Life

As you know by now, there's no "one size fits all" when it comes to forming the shape and direction of your Magnificent Life. The key is for you to tap into what you know to be true for you, not for your father or your best friend. A key question I would encourage you to consider, when you are exploring the possibilities that will open to you is, "Does this path have heart for me?"

Does a suggestion or project proposal bring a feeling of peace and ease within your body, or are you aware of some tightness or pain anywhere? Your heart can be like a beacon in the storm when you find yourself struggling with life lessons or with choices that may be outstandingly tempting and yet part of you doesn't feel right about them. Pay attention and take the time to write down any thoughts or feelings that come to you at these times, before you commit yourself.

My wish is that you will understand that within that destiny package placed in your cradle, for you and only for you, was a blessing. That blessing is that you live to appreciate and enjoy this gift of Life, for whatever length of time you are called to walk this planet. May you know that you have an ally that has always been/will always be there for you—your Soul. You already know different ways your Soul communicates with you and your homework is to keep those lines of communication open.

There will be times when you will receive messages that your life is lacking balance. These messages may come in the form of big hints from your loved ones that they aren't seeing enough of you, or a physical illness, an accident or simply a feeling of malaise. Pay attention to these clues. In the exercises that follow, you will be given some tools to help you to look at what elements you truly value and would most like to have in place in your life.

Make the most of this opportunity to record your goals so they don't get lost in the nooks and crannies of your daily life. Take a moment to make commitments that you will put into action to ensure that you will honor the most precious facets of the jewel that is you, such as your relationship with a beloved, your gifts as a writer or painter, your role as mother or father, your interest in other cultures and languages, your own health and well-being.

This is your life. What elements of it do you need to balance with other elements, such as income generation or parenthood? And be aware that as you get older, your priorities and needs will change in the swings of life. When you have balance in your life, you will find that you seldom get sick, seldom experience a feeling of loss of purpose and are seldom lonely.

Meditation—Meet Your 90-Year-Old

As my parting gift, I would like to leave with you a journey that you can take at any time, to tune in to where you are in your Magnificent Life.

When you are ready, read the paragraphs below, then put the book down and allow your imagination to take you there. Make sure you are in a quiet room where you know you will not be disturbed. Have your journal at hand and allow yourself about 20 minutes to take the journey.

You find yourself standing in a beautiful, green field. The grass is long and you see it swaying as the breeze kisses it. The field extends for a long way and in the distance you can see a mountain reaching up to the sky. For this moment though, you find yourself walking easily through the grass, across the field. You feel the warmth of the breeze on your cheeks and every now and then you smell the fragrance of a wildflower and maybe even some pine resin from nearby trees. You're wearing comfortable clothing and shoes and find yourself picking up your pace and heading towards to the mountain ahead of you. Perhaps you can see and hear the small stream nearby and you love the sight of the birds gathering by the water.

Walking, walking so comfortably. Your stride is strong and confident. There are no animals, no other humans that you can see. Just you and the soft freshness of the field.

Walking, walking. The mountain is getting closer and closer now and you begin to discern a pathway that seems to wind down from the top of the mountain. There are trees on the pathway and some big rocks. Keep on walking and enjoying the peace and feeling of well-being as you tune in to nature's gifts.

At a certain point, you become aware of a shape that looks like a human being, coming down the mountain path. Slowly. Down, down the path. And indeed, it is a person. As you keep walking, the other being is slowly getting closer, closer. You're now starting to climb up the pathway and can feel the steepness of the path. The other being is getting closer and there's a familiar look about this person. You're not far away from each other at all now and, my goodness; you take a deep breath and are quite startled to realize that this person coming down the path towards you, is you at age 90.

The person has a beautiful, welcoming smile and is beckoning to you to come and sit on a flat stone with him or her. You have no hesitation and before you know it, there you both are, looking into each other's eyes. Take your time now to just look at you at age 90. How do you look? Are you healthy and strong, or is your body ailing? What kind of energy does your 90-year-old have and what is he or she wearing? How do you feel in his or her presence?

Take your time now to talk, from your heart, with your 90-year-old. Ask him or her for any words of advice on what you need to be paying attention to in your life. How are you doing? Is there anything you need to change or consider? What advice does he or she have for you? Does he or she have any regrets that you need to know about now? Any other questions or concerns you have, now is the time to bring these up.

At a certain point, your companion will let you know that it is time for you to go your separate ways again. Take a moment to say goodbye, maybe embrace and express your thanks for this precious moment in time. And then, when you're ready, you turn around, as your companion does the same, and you start back in your different directions. Before long you're back in the grassy field, and you can barely see the older figure heading up the mountain when he or she pauses to wave. You wave back, and then take a deep breath, and you find yourself right back in your room again.

Now that you're back, pick up your pen and journal and record the messages that came through for you.

Blessings to you as you embark upon claiming your rightful inheritance—a Magnificent Life—yours.

Exercise One

Creating My Magnificent Life—Personal Goals

Refer to Appendix 6 and take your time to reflect and write down your personal goals for the Magnificent Life you are now designing.

Exercise Two

Creating My Magnificent Life—Business Goals

Do the same process as above, with Appendix 7, this time for your business goals.

Exercise Three

Creating My Magnificent Life—Commitments

In a mindful way, work with your Soul Partner on Appendix 8 now to make the sacred pacts with yourself, to which you are prepared to commit—and be accountable. Best wishes!

Appendix 1

Accountability Checklist

Areas in your personal and business life to review on a regular basis—are you 10 out of 10 in them?

Items to consider:	Daily Rating from 1 to 10					
	1	2	3	4	5	6
Dollar-Productive Activities						
Fun/Adventure/Travel						
Insurance Policies/Renewals						
Family Time/Mentoring Children						
Health/Diet						
Advocates						
New Things To Try						
Financial Review/Passive Income Streams						
Mentor/Coaching						
Music/Dance						
Business and Investment Strategies						
Hobbies						
Spiritual/Relationship with God/Meditation						
Risk and Excitement/Impossible Things						
Rest and Recuperation/Adequate Sleep						
Giving Back/Charitable Work						
Theatre and Movies						
10s						
Future Planning						
Ideal Day/Week/Year						
Friends						
Succession Planning/Trust/Will						
Self Improvement/Reading Time						
Relationships/"Get a Life" Weekends						
Birthdays—Friends and Family						
"Me Time"						
Dreams/Big Picture						
Sex						
House Maintenance						
Attention to Different Sub-Personalities (i.e., Inner Child)						

Appendix 2

Dollar-Productive Behavior I

List below the activities that you perform in your business that earn you the most income. Start with the most dollar-productive activity.

1.

2.

3.

4.

5.

6.

7.

8.

9.

10.

11.

12.

13.

14.

15.

16.

17.

18.

19.

20.

Appendix 3

Dollar-Productive Behavior II

Things I will no longer do.
List below those activities that you commit to erasing from your working day because they interfere with your dollar-productivity.

1.

2.

3.

4.

5.

6.

7.

8.

9.

10.

11.

12.

13.

14.

15.

16.

17.

18.

19.

20.

Appendix 4

Sample Day Sheet

Date: _____

6:00	Morning Ritual – Channel 22
6:30	
7:00	
7:30	Possible Breakfast with Center of Influence or Client: Channel 37
8:00	Arrive at the Office: Closed Door Time
8:30	Staff/Admin Time
9:00	Scripts and Dialogues with High-Producing Colleagues
9:30	Dollar-Productive Activity, e.g., Prospecting—Receive No Incoming Calls
10:00	
10:30	
11:00	
11:30	Follow-up—Return Incoming Calls
12:00	Lunch with a Client
13:00	Dollar-Productive Activity, e.g., Client Appointments, Negotiations, etc.
13:30	
14:00	
14:30	
15:00	
15:30	
16:00	Follow-up—Return Incoming calls
16:30	Staff /Admin Time
17:00	
17:30	
18:00	Ritual for Returning Home to Family and Personal Time: Channel 22
18:30	
19:00	

Appendix 5

Ideal Day Sheet   Date: _____

6:00

6:30

7:00

7:30

8:00

8:30

9:00

9:30

10:00

10:30

11:00

11:30

12:00

13:00

13:30

14:00

14:30

15:00

15:30

16:00

16:30

17:00

17:30

18:00

18:30

19:00

Appendix 6

Personal Goal Sheet

My three most important lifetime personal goals are:

1.

2.

3.

In five years, I visualize myself having attained the following personal goals:

1.

2.

3.

If I only had six months to live, what would be my main personal objectives?

1.

2.

3.

What activities can I complete this week to help me achieve my most important personal goals?

1.

2.

3.

Appendix 7

My Business Goal Sheet

My three most important lifetime goals for MY BUSINESS are:

1.

2.

3.

In five years, I visualize myself having attained the following goals for MY BUSINESS:

1.

2.

3.

If I only had six months to live, what would be my main objectives for MY BUSINESS?

1.

2.

3.

What activities can I complete this week to help me achieve my most important goals for MY BUSINESS?

1.

2.

3.

Appendix 8

Commitment Sheet

Commitment:

Reward/consequence:

Non-reward/consequence:

Date start: Date completed:

Commitment:

Reward/consequence:

Non-reward/consequence:

Date start: Date completed:

Commitment:

Reward/consequence:

Non-reward/consequence:

Date start: Date completed:

Appendix 9

Time Log

Your Name: _____

Write Date _____

From	To	Monday	Tuesday	Wednesday	Thursday	Friday	Saturday	Sunday
05:00	05:15							
05:15	05:30							
05:30	05:45							
05:45	06:00							
06:00	06:15							
06:15	06:30							
06:30	06:45							
06:45	07:00							
07:00	07:15							
07:15	07:30							
07:30	07:45							
07:45	08:00							
08:00	08:15							
08:15	08:30							
08:30	08:45							
08:45	09:00							
09:00	09:15							
09:15	09:30							
09:30	09:45							
09:45	10:00							
10:00	10:15							

10:15	10:30	10:45	11:00	11:15	11:30	11:45	12:00	12:15	12:30	12:45	13:00	13:15	13:30	13:45	14:00	14:15	14:30	14:45	15:00	15:15	15:30	15:45	16:00	16:15	16:30	16:45	17:00	
10:30	10:45	11:00	11:15	11:30	11:45	12:00	12:15	12:30	12:45	13:00	13:15	13:30	13:45	14:00	14:15	14:30	14:45	15:00	15:15	15:30	15:45	16:00	16:15	16:30	16:45	17:00	17:15	

Appendix 9 (continued)

Time Log

Your Name: _____

	17:15	17:30	17:45	18:00	18:15	18:30	18:45	19:00	19:15	19:30	19:45	20:00	20:15	20:30	20:45	21:00	21:15	21:30	21:45	22:00	22:15	22:30	22:45
17:30																							
17:45																							
18:00																							
18:15																							
18:30																							
18:45																							
19:00																							
19:15																							
19:30																							
19:45																							
20:00																							
20:15																							
20:30																							
20:45																							
21:00																							
21:15																							
21:30																							
21:45																							
22:00																							
22:15																							
22:30																							
22:45																							
23:00																							

As an internationally recognized Business/Life Coach/Mentor, Dr. Fred Grosse teaches, guides and inspires achievers on how to create a Magnificent Life bountifully funded by Dollar Productive Activities and investments. Dr Fred's key theme is, "LIFE is primary and WORK funds life." He is not only sought after as a keynote speaker and trainer at conferences worldwide; he is also personally available for corporate/partnership and individual/group coaching. He and his wife Victoria also conduct Boutique "100" conferences in sacred places around the world.

Free Gifts from Dr. Fred

Be sure to download Victoria's "Birthing the Dream" meditation CD on www.drfredgrosse.com.

If you'd like to be on our bi-weekly emailing list receiving Dr. Fred's teaching parable, please send your name and email address to: inst4mom@drfredgrosse.com

---

Dr. Fred Grosse is a business / life coach and mentor to high-performing entrepreneurs, CEOs, business owners, corporations and salespeople around the world. According to Dr. Fred, "Success is not just about achieving in business. It is about discovering your own unique life's purpose and cultivating a meaningful life that is enjoyed to the fullest."

Services

Daily Accountability Programs with Dr Fred
Dr. Fred offers a new, daily accountability program – **the 1K Club** – with a very limited number of places available, this program provides for daily email contact with Dr. Fred and telephone contact three times a month.

One-on-One Coaching with Dr. Fred Grosse
"Invest in Yourself" ... with telephone or in-person private coaching with Dr. Fred—specially priced packages for Private Individual Coaching and Corporate Consulting.

Speaking Engagements and Corporate Consulting
Dr. Fred's clients are luminaries of the real estate, financial, automotive and other key industries. A recognized international speaker, Dr. Fred's dynamic presentations empower top producers to stretch beyond their comfort zones, rediscover passion, and realize tangible, magnificent, life-changing results.

Wealth³ Mastermind Groups
Wealth³ is a limited-enrollment, extraordinary mentoring program personally facilitated by Dr. Fred Grosse. Over the course of a year, groups of 25 to 40 individuals meet with Dr Grosse four times in 2-day sessions, receiving the **in-depth coaching** necessary to transform counter-productive behaviors and belief patterns into permanent **life altering assets**.

Products

Black Belt of the Mind
Available in CD format or as a set of tapes, in this program Dr. Fred will teach you how to fine-tune both your conscious and unconscious patterns to help you effectively achieve continuing and increasing work satisfaction, wealth and good health.

Black Belt of the Mind: Part II
In this sequel to the popular *Black Belt of the Mind* Dr. Fred shares his breathtakingly simple techniques for building what you know into the habits that will provide financial independence and a magnificent life.

Balanced Living
In this interview with Howard Brinton, Dr. Fred will take you on a journey of self-discovery that will empower your business and enhance your personal life.

All products are available in either audio cassette or CD formats.
To view all of Dr. Fred's products please visit his website www.drfredgrosse.com

To find out more about Dr. Fred, please call:
USA (602) 956-6893 • Fax (602) 956-6131
Australia and New Zealand (64) 3 341-5690 • Fax (64) 3 341-5695
E-mail: inst4mom@drfredgrosse.com